"Are we ashamed of our devotion to the cause of Christ? If so, we have allowed others to define who we are as believers and allowed boundaries to be placed on the Gospel."
- Gary Adams

BREAKING MEDIOCRITY
Unlocking Your Potential

TRIBUTE PUBLISHING
2017

Copyright © 2017
Tribute Publishing, LLC.
Frisco, Texas U.S.A

Breaking Mediocrity
First Edition June 2017

All Worldwide Rights Reserved
ISBN: 978-0-9982860-5-1

All Rights Reserved. No part of this book may be reproduced, stored in a retrieval system, or transmitted, in any form, or by any means, electronic, mechanical, recorded, photocopied, or otherwise, without the prior written permission of the copyright owner, except by a reviewer who may quote brief passages in a review.

This book is dedicated to one of the
most amazing people in my life,
my wife of over 53 years,
Ruth Sturtevant Adams,
without whose love, encouragement, and
sacrifice, this book would not
have been written.

CONTENTS

Prologue xiii

Chapter 1 – A Dynamic Church 1
   Just What is the Church? 2
   The Awakening Church 4
   The Power of the Church 5
   The Church in Action 8
   A Solution for the Church 10
   The Influence of the Church 12
   God is Shaping His Church 13

Chapter 2 – A Dynamic Walk 17
   A Personal Walk 19
   Walking in Faith 24
   Walking in the Spirit 27

Chapter 3 – Prayer Dynamics 37
   Praying and Abiding 39
   Prayer and Righteousness 41
   God's Holiness 42
   God's Sovereignty 45
   Persistent Prayer 51
   Consistent Prayer 55
   Commitment to Prayer 57
   Communion in Prayer 61
   Influence of Prayer 62

Chapter 4 – Dynamic Relationships 67
   Unity in Relationships 69
   Vulnerability in Relationships.................................... 70
   Loss of Fellowship.. 71
   Healing in Relationships 73
   Restoration in Relationships 76
   Forgiveness in Relationships 76

Chapter 5 – Dynamic Leadership 79
   Humility... 80
   Conviction... 82
   Courage 83

Chapter 6 – Dynamic Faith 87

Epilogue 99

About the Author 103

Prologue

Who am I? I am one man on a mission. One whose heart longs to see an end-time church arise to the glorious destiny God has ordained. I am one with a fire in his belly and a passion for seeing God's glory in His church and His people. I am one who yearns to see the church become a healthy and vibrant church that is bold and determined to advance and not retreat in the face of religious giants seeking to rob God of His glory in the earth. I am one who prays that the church, like the young shepherd boy David, will find smooth stones, take up a slingshot, and challenge the giant seeking to intimidate and destroy the church of the Living God. I am praying for a persevering church, a triumphant church that brings glory to God. I am one who believes that a Warrior God has declared that He will have a glorious church without spot or wrinkle, washed in the blood of the Lamb.

This book is written for all types of people. First, it is for those who are already in agreement and accept this writing as an affirmation to what God has already spoken to them. Their hearts have already been stirred, and they, like many other pilgrims, are on a quest to find the best that God has for them. They are like trailblazers; those who will forge ahead, having counted the cost, who shun peril, and who determinedly press on toward the prize of the high calling in Christ Jesus. It is also for those who are curious, perhaps even casual seekers, but those whose appetite has been whet for something more than what they've had. For them, this writing may serve as instruction in areas of life and service that they never realized were available to them. For them, this book may be as a seed planted. My prayer is that the seed will sprout, take root, and ultimately bring forth good fruit in their lives.

My desire is that this writing will become an inspiration, a challenge, and encouragement for every reader to go on with God. Go to a new level. Go to a place with God you've never been before. Why are you waiting? Be one with a heart, a heart that seeks after the Living God, a heart that is not content to be lukewarm. Let yours be a heart that is not hardened, but one totally yielded to God that He can say that you have drawn near to him. He will draw near to you. Don't let your hearts be far removed. He is calling for you to come with Him to a new level of grace and glory.

My purpose is both to inspire and provoke God's people individually and the church collectively to awaken to and exercise the spiritual law of dynamics. Jesus is coming for a victorious, triumphant church. It will be a dynamic church. The chapters of this book present Biblical forms of dynamics. This writing is not intended to be an academic exercise, but rather a spiritual challenge to rise higher, to move to a new level in God, a place perhaps not yet attained. It is an exhortation to break out of the business-as-usual mindset that is pervasive in today's world. If the Church is ever to get out of a decline, shake off a reputation for being irrelevant, and become a world-changing entity, it must embrace God's law of dynamics. Now is the time!

Chapter 1

A Dynamic Church

Is the modern church of today about to crash and burn, or is this just more "the sky is falling" rhetoric? There are those who believe that Christianity and the evangelical church are in a steady decline. They suggest that the effectiveness, viability, and cultural relevance of the church has steadily decreased. Pastors and church leaders sometimes share these concerns with their peers, and it is not uncommon for these concerns to be brought up for discussion. It was at a pastor's meeting, focused on these issues that I realized just how serious these concerns were. In this meeting, one major concern expressed was that church attendance was in decline for many of the churches or parishes represented. Several of the speakers referenced studies and surveys that they had discovered while doing research on the issues. Some studies spoke of the church in terms of being irrelevant, apathetic, or complacent.

Arguably, these studies may reflect the current trend for some mainline denominations, but do not necessarily represent the condition of the church universally. One might

Chapter 1 – A Dynamic Church

ask why the church is in decline. Could it be that the accusation of cultural irrelevance and forms of religious institutionalism are interconnected and have not only left people with a spiritual void, but also with a major disconnect between everyday life? Could it be that the church exhibits a mere form of godliness but denies the power of God to effect change in people? Are we not building the church according to God's plan? These and many other questions hang heavy over many ministers today. In attempts to break the cycle of decline, we tend to invent, and, in some instances, imitate, all manner of church growth initiatives. We seem to have a program for everybody and everything. We are desperately looking to keep up with social demands of a new generation of churchgoers, trying to appeal to every level of society, often compromising our convictions. Yet, we are in decline. Sadly, many ministries have failed, ministers have become discouraged and left the ministry altogether, and congregants have become disillusioned and abandoned their faith for lack of relevance by the church. The good news is that God has a solution to these issues.

Just What Is the Church?
When I speak of the church, I am not referencing the institution, but rather the people who make up the church, a universal body of *believers*, the living stones, or those who are being built together as an holy habitation for God. The church is not just bricks and mortar, nor is it merely an organization. <u>The church is people</u>. We who believe are the church. As Pastor Jerry Bernard sang in one of his songs many years ago, "The

Chapter 1 – A Dynamic Church

house of God is built with people bricks; side by side, different kinds together."

In the early days of ministry, while I was pastoring a growing church, a ministerial acquaintance would frequently drop by my office to chat. Invariably, he would begin to lecture me on all the problems with the church in America and was clear to point out things that "were not of God." After some time, I began to become weary of always hearing "what the church is not." Finally, out of exasperation, I told him, "I am tired of hearing about what the church is not. If you can't explain to me what the church is, stop telling me what it is not!" He rarely brought the subject up again. My purpose in writing on this matter is not to declare what the church is not, but rather to proclaim boldly what the church is. While I certainly don't have all the answers to these and other issues, I do believe God has declared that He will have a triumphant church. In Haggai 2:3 the question is asked, "Who of you is left who saw this house in its former glory? How does it look to you now? Does it not seem to you like nothing?" (NIV). Honestly, I believe we could ask the same questions today. What is the church? How should the church look? How should the church conduct itself? In recent years, having visited many churches around the nation, I realized that something has dramatically changed in the past thirty or forty years. In the late 60's, God was moving in such a way that many people had a deep hunger for God. In the church I attended at that time, the prayer rooms would fill over an hour before services began with people eager to pray. People would come to the church to pray in the early hours of the morning before going to their workplace. Worship was not

Chapter 1 – A Dynamic Church

so regimented and sermons not so hurried that the Holy Spirit would move in almost every meeting. Many people were being saved and baptized in those days. The church was growing exponentially, and there was a tremendous spirit of expectancy among people, so much so, that most people did not want to miss a service. The Jesus Movement, as it came to be known, brought thousands into the Kingdom of God. There was a fresh outpouring of God's Spirit, and, while not all participated nor even appreciated this move, the religious landscape changed. Inevitably, God moved in amazing ways in mainline denominations as well.

The Awakening Church
A move of God took place in Wilmore, Kentucky at Asbury College in 1970. This was one of several moves of God that would positively impact the Church of our day; it was an awakening. It began in a morning chapel service that was scheduled for 50 minutes. A powerful presence of God swept through the chapel. Students began to fill the chapel and few wanted to leave. The entire campus was affected, and the chapel service continued non-stop for weeks. Ultimately, the effects of the revival at Asbury College spread across the nation and around the world.

I was myself a Bible college student at the time in Florida, and news of the Asbury revival quickly reached our little college, sparking a spiritual hunger among our students. The ongoing effect of this move of God resulted in many lives changed to the glory of God. My life was changed. My view of church shifted to becoming proactive in ministry. It seemed that the church at the time was in a quagmire of stale religiosity and empty rhetoric. Sermons often had a historical

Chapter 1 – A Dynamic Church

slant where what used to be was preached about, but little was preached about where the church should be headed. Yesterday's manna was old and the awakening church was hungry for something fresh from God.

Another fresh move of God did occur. It was known as "The Brownsville Revival." It was centered in Pensacola, Florida, but influence from it swept across the United States. There were many accounts of this revival, and, as with most revival reports, there were advocates and adversaries, but nobody could deny the fact that many lives were changed. This revival began on Father's Day, June 18, 1995, at the Brownsville Assembly of God Church in Pensacola, Florida. It was reported that more than four million people attended the revival meetings from its beginnings in 1995 to around 2000. Additionally, it was said that nearly 200,000 people claimed they gave their lives to Jesus, and by fall of the year 2000 more than 1,000 individuals who experienced the revival were taking classes at the Brownsville Revival School of Ministry. Thousands of pastors visited Brownsville and returned to their home congregations, leading to an outbreak of mini-revivals that helped the Assemblies of God denomination recover from what some saw as a denominational decline. Brownsville Revival. (2016, November 9). Retrieved from *Wikipedia, The Free Encyclopedia.*
(https://en.wikipedia.org/wiki/Brownsville_Revival)

The Power of the Church

Early in my ministry, I researched the Greek word for "power," which in Greek is the word "dunamis." I believed that I was preaching a powerful message, but also knew that I wanted more than an occasional demonstration of power.

Chapter 1 – A Dynamic Church

I believed God wanted to demonstrate the power of His word, dynamic to His glory. Little did I know that what the Lord would reveal to me through a study of the Book of Acts would bring a new dynamic to my ministry, my family, and my prayer life. The word dunamis dropped in my spirit like a depth-charge. I knew it was significant, but suddenly the depth-charge detonated and brought about a massive explosion in my spirit. What I discovered was that the word dunamis also had further meaning. The word dunamis is the root for words such as dynamite, which, as we know, is an explosive power, and it is also foundational to defining the word dynamo, which is a perpetuated power.

Upon further research, I found that dunamis was also the root word for dynamic. I thought to myself that the power of the Holy Spirit upon us might not only be an explosive type power or continual power perpetuated by the Holy Spirit, although I knew these were tested applications, but what would it mean to become dynamic? I felt compelled to research further the meaning of the word "dynamic." According to Merriam Webster's Dictionary, dynamic is defined as: *of or relating to energy, motion, or physical force.* These are the three essential elements of dynamics. Consider aerodynamics for example. If all power (*energy*) to the engines are shut down, the plane may glide for a while, but it is going down. The same holds true of electrodynamics, hydrodynamics, or any other form of dynamic. If there is no *motion*, there is no dynamic. Likewise, if there is no energy or *force*, there is no dynamic. As I pondered these various types of dynamics, it became clear to me that there are also spiritual dynamics. Like any other dynamic, spiritual dynamics must also have the three essential elements.

Chapter 1 – A Dynamic Church

I began an extensive study of Scripture to identify different forms of spiritual dynamics. The more I searched the Scripture, the more obvious it was to me that dynamics are an integral part of our spiritual walk. Spiritual dynamics emanate from God himself. He is the very dynamic of all that He has asked us to do or be. The Bible tells us that without Him, we can do nothing, but also tells us that through Him, we can do anything. (John 15:5; Matthew 19:26) To become a truly dynamic Christian, we must acknowledge that it is only through Him that we can accomplish anything for His glory.

Looking back at the founding of the church in the Book of Acts, we see a powerful, vibrant expression of faith, including God's favor and blessing upon His people. Many people were getting saved and baptized; people were being added to the church daily. Sick people were healed, the dead were raised, and people were freed from demonic control. The church met often and there was a strong sense of unity and togetherness among the people. The church was a dynamic force. God was honoring His presence among them, empowering them by the Holy Spirit to perform miracles, signs, and wonders. Spiritual gifts were in full operation, and people were in awe of what was happening in their midst. By all Biblical standards, the church at inception was dynamic. The promise of God that they would receive power when the Holy Spirit came on them was all the promise they needed. God not only defined "what" the church is to be but also instructs us on "how" to be that church. The word 'power' as used in Acts 1:8 is from the Greek and is defined in Strong's Concordance: *dunamis* (miraculous) power, might, strength. The church has been strengthened in faith and edified by the promise of God's power contained in this verse. This power is not only available to the church representing the corporate Body of Christ, but also to every born again, spirit-baptized believer as well.

There are those who would argue that the days of miracles are no longer, that signs and wonders were relegated to the early church. Certainly, no serious student of the Bible would deny the fact that miracles, signs, and wonders took place as recorded in the book of Acts. To a large extent, it was the signs, wonders, and miracles that contributed to the explosive growth of the early church. But some would say, "that was for then, not now." However, there is no substantial evidence to validate claims that the days of miracles are over. On the contrary, miracles, signs, and wonders do still occur, as supported by many witnesses whose personal testimonies confirm such wondrous accounts. Nobody can reasonably argue the personal testimony of another person. One may not believe another's story, but one can't simply say, "That didn't happen to you!" In almost a half-century of ministry, I have personally known and been involved with many who have experienced miracles spiritually, emotionally, physically, and financially. It is amazing how God delights to be involved in our lives.

The Church in Action
Having been convinced that we, as individuals, and the church, collectively, should be dynamic, I began to search the Bible for clues on how to become a dynamic person and how to effectively transfer that message and vision to others. So many of those we consider to be great men and women of faith left us an example of what it means to live an energized,

Chapter 1 – A Dynamic Church

enthusiastic life. Hebrews chapter 11 identifies many of those people such as Abel, Enoch, Noah, Abraham, Sarah, and others. It is of particular importance to us as individuals to grasp and understand the faith life of those who've gone before us since the church will never be any more influential than the people who comprise it.

The lost world needs a demonstration! Why should scoffers mockingly ask where our God is? There is a lost world waiting to see if the God we preach is real. There are those who have yet to acknowledge their need for a savior because it has yet to be proven to them that they have a need. It seems that for all our preaching and teaching, there remains a need for demonstration of the gospel. In other words, we will never be a dynamic entity unless we can personally and collectively demonstrate the Gospel. The Bible talks about those who have a form of godliness, but deny the power of God. (2 Timothy 3:5) Further, the Scripture states that we are to be doers of the word and not just hearers because if we are anything less than doers, we have deceived ourselves. (James 1:22) In other words, we have become masters at talking a good talk, but bearing little fruit. Much has been said about the church having potential. What does that mean? Potential as defined in the dictionary simply means "existing in possibility." God has made it clear that He wants a dynamic church not just in existing possibility, but in actuality. Jesus expressed this clearly. That was clear when He said, "the works that I do shall you do also, and greater works than these shall you do..." (John 14:12) Even if one denies the notion that this promise applies to anyone outside the original disciples, there is no denying the fact that Jesus stated such with specific intent. He never spoke what the Father did not give Him. If this were God's heart, then, it

Chapter 1 – A Dynamic Church

would mean that God gave not only a message, but specific instructions to His disciples. This became one of the primary messages conveyed to the fledgling New Testament Church. If, in fact, that was the foundation upon which the New Testament Church was laid, how could we now expect any less? If anything, the church should demonstrate the dynamic power of the Gospel as much, if not more, than it did at inception.

The church spoken of in the Book of Acts was a powerful church. They devoted themselves to good teaching, to fellowship, and to prayer. Awesome signs and wonders were evident in the church and the result of such a ministry was that people were being saved and the church was growing daily. (Acts 2:42-47) That is a picture of a dynamic church. Without question, the church of today has the same potential. Whether or not we rise up to our potential will determine the effectiveness of the modern-day church. Are we willing to accept God's standard for success or will we insist on acceptance of man's definition of a successful church? If we use the Scripture as a standard measure, we must ask ourselves if we are achieving the same results as the early church. Do we yearn for and expect God to reveal His power and glory in the church? Do we anticipate wonders and miraculous signs being done today? There are parts of the world where God is moving in such a way through His church.

A Solution for the Church

Accounts such as those regarding the church in the Book of Acts, pose a challenge to those who yearn to once again see

Chapter 1 – A Dynamic Church

God's glory and power restored to His church. The challenge is to have faith and passion to see the church of our day become all that God wants it to be. For this to happen, there must be pastors and leaders in the church who will not settle for mediocrity. These are those who are not content with a 'status quo' or 'business as usual' approach to ministry. There is a generation today like this. Even now, coming out of the shadows of political correctness and religious academics are those who will not settle for less than God's best in the church. There is a young generation beginning to rise within the ranks of the church. They recognize hypocrisy, sense what is right spiritually, and they are choosing the sacred over the profane. They will be pillars in the church of our day.

I've had the privilege of having known many missionaries. One of those was an extraordinary minister and Bible teacher. He made a tremendous impact in my life as he shared personal stories with me about his missionary experiences. I was awed by the dedication of this man and others like him who willingly blazed a trail for others to follow. These people were "doers." The Bible admonishes us to not only be a hearer, but a doer. He told me of natives in one country who were ready to renounce their fetish worship and follow God. The people were distraught because they were faced with giving up their ways of worship in order to enter into a new religion. For them, it was a religion which had not been tried by their people. They had heard the stories of the Christian faith, but their reluctance to readily accept this new religion was because they had not seen with their own eyes, a demonstration of the Christian faith. My friend went on to explain that the power of God began to manifest among the natives, and many miracles, signs, and wonders followed, including a person being raised from the dead, healing of leprosy, and other deadly diseases among the people. God used his faithful missionaries to demonstrate the power of His dynamic gospel, and as a result, entire villages committed their lives to Christ.

The Influence of the Church

Throughout the history of the church, there have been dynamic ministers whom God has used to impact the world. The Book of Acts details the dynamic ministry of the apostles who not only preached with passion and conviction, but also demonstrated their message through God using them to perform signs, wonders, and miracles which became foundational to the church. It is clear from the Scriptures that God intended His church to have an influence on the earth. Historically, there are times when the church has had more influence than at others, but the plan of God has not changed. During my lifetime, I have witnessed powerful revivals and extraordinary moves of God's Spirit, often accompanied by signs, wonders, and miracles. It was, after all, the great commission that Jesus gave to His disciples to go into all the world preaching, healing the sick, cleansing lepers, raising the dead, and casting out evil spirits. (Matthew 10:8) This was not only the platform for the church in the Book of Acts, but serves as the example and pattern for the church of today. Any other attempts to create God-given influence apart from God's plan not only represents the height of man's arrogance, but is doomed for failure.

Chapter 1 – A Dynamic Church

Our prayer is that the church today will once again rise to a place of societal prominence and position of influence.

God is Shaping His Church
God relates to and interacts with mankind on several different levels. We find His interest in each of us individually, as a family, a faith-community, and as a nation. Note the progression; first is the individual, next the family. Remember, the family will be no stronger than the individual members of that family. Then comes the faith-community or church. The faith community is made of individuals and families. Strong families make a strong Church. And last He addresses the Nation. A Nation will never be more godly than the individuals, families, and faith communities that represent the population of that Nation. "Blessed is that nation whose God is the Lord" (Ps.33:12).

The Book of Revelation describes several types of churches. I want to mention two of those which I believe parallel two types of churches in our present day. The first is found in Revelation 3:14-19. The church of Laodicea was the picture of an apostate church. They represent a church taken by a spirit of amusement and entertainment. The word amuse as defined in the dictionary can mean to "not think." The Archaic form of the word amuse means, "To divert the attention so as to deceive." (Webster's) To entertain, which is synonymous with amuse, means, "diverting; to keep, hold, or maintain in the mind." The church of Laodicea was the only church mentioned in the Book

Chapter 1 – A Dynamic Church

of Revelation that was charged with being lukewarm. This church was deceived. They thought that they were wealthy and didn't have need of anything. However, God's view of them was different. His view of them was that they were wretched and poor, and were not even aware of such. There is a parallel to that church in our present day. The church that is given to amusement and entertainment is often a lukewarm or mediocre church, which means it is neither good nor bad. There is nothing dynamic about a lukewarm church. The Lord makes clear the unacceptability of being lukewarm, saying that it would be better to be either hot or cold. The good news is that the Lord loves His church, even the lukewarm church, but He wants the deception broken from them; He is calling this church to repentance.

The second church I want to mention is the church of Philadelphia. (Rev.3:7-10). I call this church the enthused church. They were a dynamic representation of God's plan for His church in the earth. The word "enthuse" by ancient Greek definition comes from a root formation en-theos which means "God possessed." It means, "A belief in special revelations of the Holy Spirit," and can also mean "religious fanatacism." Historically, it has been the enthused church that pursues God with a passion and with great determination intercedes for God to enable and empower the church to His glory. The term "fanatic" has often been used in a derogotory sense to identify those who seem to be overboard in their beliefs. The

Chapter 1 – A Dynamic Church

more I've pondered this, the more I am convinced that being a fanatic isn't necessarily bad. If you think about it, we are all fanatical about something. According to the Merriam Webster Dictionary, fanatic is defined as: very or overly enthusiastic or devoted. The word was applied to members of certain Protestant groups who argued for their belief with excessive enthusiasm, acting as if they were divinely inspired. Eventually, *fanatic* was applied to anyone who showed extreme devotion to a cause.

With this definition in mind, do you think that we, as inspired by the Holy Spirit, and enthused (God possessed), should not express our beliefs with great enthusiasm? Isn't that the purpose of being a disciple of Jesus? What did people think of the woman Jesus ministered to at the well in Samaria? She immediately went and enthusiastically told the entire city what Jesus had done for her. (John 4:1-42) Are we ashamed of our devotion to the cause of Christ? If so, we have allowed others to define who we are as believers and allowed boundaries to be placed on the Gospel. In doing so we have limited, or at least neutralized, the effect of the Gospel from impacting the lives of those around us for fear of being considered a fanatic. This does not give a believer license to be rude or obnoxious, but neither does it excuse us from unenthusiastically presenting a watered-down Gospel that has no power to effect change in a person's life. The world around us is waiting to see a demonstration. They want to know that what we present is better than what they already have. If you are not enthused, how can you expect anybody else to want what you offer?

Chapter 1 – A Dynamic Church

Chapter 2

A Dynamic Walk

> He that saith he abideth in him ought himself also so
> to walk, even as he walked.
> (1 John 2:6 KJV)

What is so important about defining our walk? The answer to that is that we fashion ourselves after those we walk with, or follow. I remember as a child, trying to be just like my Dad. I wanted to walk like he did, talk like him, and be like him. The Bible teaches us that we are to be imitators of God. (Ephesians 5:1-2) To do that means that we need to be more like Jesus. He was God's perfect Son; so if we want to please God, we must be more like Jesus. We want to walk like Him, talk like He does, and pray like He prayed. The more we walk in His ways, the more we will understand His heart. As the opening verse to this chapter states, it is not only possible, but expected that we walk like He walked.

The Bible has much to say about walking. Beginning in Genesis, we see that God walked with Adam and Eve in the

Chapter 2 – A Dynamic Walk

Garden of Eden. Enoch walked with God, and one can only imagine what an amazing walk he had, as he just walked right on into God's presence where God took him. There are many other examples throughout the Bible which identify both those who had a good walk with God, and those who walked perversely, or in darkness.

One illustration of a dynamic walk is that of Noah. The Scripture tells us that Noah walked with God. That is a wonderful testimony. It is interesting to note that in several places in the Scripture, the idea of being perfect or upright is directly related to God's ways. Abram was ninety-nine years old when God spoke to him and told him to walk before Him. (Genesis 17:1)

To walk is to take action. One must exert energy, force, and motion to walk, which means that walking is dynamic. Walking can mean different things to different people, depending on the context in which the word is used. We can walk many paths, take many directions, and direct our steps to take us to desired destinations. A spiritual walk is also dynamic. To walk with God, to follow His leading, and to walk in His paths carries us toward a destination filled with eternal values and consequences. We have a choice to follow Him or not. We can walk "in the spirit," or we can opt to walk "in the flesh." Scripture tells us that if we walk according to the flesh, we shall reap destruction. On the other hand, to walk in the Spirit leads to life. (Galatians 6:8) We often hear or read idioms and metaphors concerning walking. For example, "You

Chapter 2 – A Dynamic Walk

have to walk before you run," "Let's take a walk down memory lane," or to "walk a mile in someone's shoes," to name just a few. God does not force our walk, but expects that we will walk in His ways. Walking in covenant with Him ensures covenant blessings for us.

A Personal Walk
The importance of our walk with God concerns our welfare and the welfare of our children. God tested His people to see if they would walk in His ways and to see if they would teach those ways to their children. King David was a "man after God's own heart" and his descendants were admonished to walk as their father David had walked. God's promise was to bless the families of those who walked as David did. (I Kings 9:4-5, I Kings 11:33, 38)

There were other men and women of God who walked with God in such a way that not only their children were affected, but future generations as well. The impact one's personal walk with the Lord has on others can have eternal ramifications. Joshua was a good example of a man who knew how to walk with God in many ways. He had exemplified his servant heart while serving with Moses for many years. During that time, through trials and testing, Joshua's character began to surface. His loyalty to Moses was obvious. His courage was without question, and his ability to lead God's people was affirmed by the people themselves. Joshua influenced not only the children of Israel, but also his own family. It was because of his walk with God that he could boldly declare that, as far as he was concerned, both he and his family would follow God.

Chapter 2 – A Dynamic Walk

God trusted Abraham to teach his children. What God had to say about him remains a testimony throughout the ages for all. God said that he knew Abraham well enough to know that he would train his children to follow after God. It was because of his walk in faithfulness that God made a covenant with him. It is because of that covenant that we have promise of eternal life through Jesus. Abraham is the father of the faithful. Faithful Abraham was blessed by faithful God. In his humanness, Abraham stumbled in his walk with God on occasion, but he was constant in his faithfulness to the extent that it was through his lineage that Jesus would come, and all the nations of the earth would be blessed.

Is walking with God as did men and women of old still possible today? Could it be that God wants to bless us in direct correlation to our keeping in step with Him? The Scripture states that in the last days, the ungodly will walk in their own ways, following their own lusts. (2 Peter 3:3) Walking contrary to God's ways is described in Scripture as walking according to the ways of worldliness. By "worldliness," I am speaking of a worldly, secular mindset. It is a mindset that is often set in opposition to the nature, ways, and Word of God. This can be seen today in much of the philosophical mindset that has been termed as "secular-humanism." Secular-humanism is living according to man's dictates more than walking in God's ways. The point here is not a political statement, but rather a spiritual challenge to all professing believers to embrace and walk in God's ways.

The importance of such a walk is given in the 13th chapter of Genesis. There we find two men walking together in the

Chapter 2 – A Dynamic Walk

promise of God, Abram, and his nephew Lot. Abram had already received tremendous covenant promises from God (Gen.12:1-3). Abram and Lot both had become rich in livestock, silver, and gold. Coming to Bethel, which means "House of God," Abram calls on God.

One of the first things recorded happening to Abram after he called on the Lord, came in the form of family strife. There was not enough pasture for all the livestock owned by himself and his nephew Lot. It became such an issue that Abram addressed Lot and made a plea with him to end the strife. Abram then made a choice that would have eternal significance. He offered Lot the privilege to look over the land, and to choose the area of land he wanted for himself. Lot looked toward the plain of Jordan and noted that it was well watered everywhere, like the garden of the Lord so he chose for himself all the plain of Jordan (Gen.13:11). Then Abram had another word from the Lord, promising him all the land, as far as he could see, from the north, south, east and west. This is the covenant land of Israel. Sadly, Lot's choice included the cities of Sodom and Gomorrah, which were later destroyed by fire due to wickedness. Lot lost his wife, family members, and all his family possessions due to his poor choices.

Reflecting upon this account, one might consider the consequences of the choice these two men made. The path each chose impacted their journey with God. Abram walked with God, and his path in life bears witness to his walk. Lot, on the other hand, took a path that seemed good to him, but it ended up being a path of destruction and heartache. Abram

Chapter 2 – A Dynamic Walk

already had experience in not obeying God's leading. He had journeyed into Egypt, and even though there is no recorded rebuke or displeasure from God for doing so, Egypt was not to be the land God was going to give him. He grew wealthy there, but that was not the ultimate destination for him. God brought Abram back to Bethel, where he had been at the beginning, between Bethel and Ai. The name Bethel means "House of God," and Ai means, "a heap of ruins." So we find Abram back at the place of the altar, with the House of God on one side and a heap of ruins on the other. He now has to make another choice concerning which way to journey.

Has there been instances in your life when you knew you had a promise from God and you began moving obediently in the direction you believed He was leading you, only to encounter heavy opposition? It may have come as family strife, financial crisis, social disconnection, physical illness, or one of any number of spiritual, physical, emotional, or financial problems. These are tactics that can hinder your walk with God. In these instances, allow God to renew your passion, love, and enthusiasm for Him. One sure way to examine where you are in the faith is to ask yourself if you are as enthused today as you were the day you came to the Lord. If you are not, ask Him for help and He will help restore you. (Psalm 51:12) He wants to bless you, fill you with His presence, and renew you. Don't confuse your success and achievement in life with your testimony. There is much more to your story. There was a time in my life when, feeling as though I was bound by a "performance bond," I felt that I had

Chapter 2 – A Dynamic Walk

to do something in order to be pleasing to God. I mistakenly thought that if I could do enough, God would be more pleased with me. The thought was, that the more I did, the more successful I was as a believer. I was struggling to please God, both as a person and as a minister of the Gospel. God wants us to know that He approves of and loves us for who we are, not just because we do something for Him. While praying about this I thought, "God, how can we be pleasing to you when we are doing nothing?" Almost instantly, I had a distinct impression, "That's the problem! You think you have <u>to do</u>, in order <u>to be</u>. If you will become who I've called you to be, you will do what I have called you to do." To "will" speaks of one's *desire* and to "do" speaks of *ability* to do.

God not only <u>gives us the *desire*</u> to do His will, but <u>the ability to do what pleases Him</u>. (emphasis added) (Psalm 37:4; Philippians 2:13; Hebrews 13:21) That revelation can bring us a new measure of freedom. We can be free from the pressure to perform and we can please God just by being. Doing is the easy part. It's our becoming more like Jesus and being more conformed to His image that make us dynamic. It is then we realize the power of living, moving, and having our being in Him. No longer is our walk a mere perfunctory exercise, hoping that we can somehow muster up enough points with God for Him to approve of us. Doing these things we may appear successful to others, and even convince ourselves of a measure of success, but God knows, and more importantly, we are able to know when something is amiss in our relationship with Him. We may struggle on our part,

Chapter 2 – A Dynamic Walk

just trying to please God. But like Cain, we may be bringing the fruit of our own labor to the Lord. There is nothing dynamic about that.

Walking in Faith
The Gospel of Matthew (14:29-34) provides an excellent illustration and life-lesson of a walk of faith. In this account, Jesus had been walking on water to His disciples. Peter, ever impetuous, sees Jesus walking on the water and says to Him, "Tell me to come to you on the water." When Jesus said "Come," Peter stepped out on the water but fearing the wind, he began to sink. He cried out to the Lord to save him. Although Jesus did save him, He questioned Peter. "Why did you doubt?" One lesson to be gleaned from this story is this: when you ask to come closer to Jesus, be prepared for a supernatural walk of faith. We've learned from Scripture that "The just shall live by faith," and also, that it is impossible to please God without faith.

To walk in faith requires implicit trust in the Lord. The old hymn "Trust and Obey" begins with these words: "When we walk with the Lord in the light of His Word, What a glory He sheds on our way!" The beloved chorus then states, "Trust and obey, for there's no other way…" There is a truth declared through this hymn. Trust and obedience are two key factors in walking with the Lord. They are an absolute necessity to walking in faith in everyday situations and practical ways. The Christian life will never be dynamic apart from this faith walk.

To obey the Lord and walk in faith we must hear, or perceive, what He is saying to us. Jesus said, "My sheep know My

Chapter 2 – A Dynamic Walk

voice," so we know we have ears to hear what He is saying to us. Just as children may recognize the voice of their parents, they still must learn what the parents mean when they speak. Many Christians recognize the Lord's voice, but don't always understand clearly what He is saying. God not only wants us to know His voice, but to know that He is willing to teach us to understand His leading.

One important lesson in hearing and obeying happened early in my ministry. I had started a ministry in a small storefront building near the Campus of a major university in our city. It wasn't too long until we began to outgrow the facility and needed additional space for various aspects of ministry. Next door to the storefront was a large, two-story, English-Tudor style house. I thought that would be an excellent addition to our ministry space. At the time, the house was empty. Peering through the windows, I could tell that the beautiful old house had been empty for some time. It was completely furnished, but all the furniture was covered. I had not seen anybody enter or visit the house for the several months our church had been next door. There were no signs, phone numbers, or other means to determine who I might be able to contact concerning the house. I asked one of the men of our church to join me on the front porch of the house so that I could get his thoughts on whether or not he felt the house would be suitable for our ministry. He joined me, and together, we peered through the windows all around the house. It seemed to both of us that the house would be well-suited for our needs. We joined together in fervent prayer that day, and we asked the Lord to provide this house for our ministry. We both had an assurance that God had heard our prayer and we believed that He would do a miracle for us. After we prayed, I began a search to find the owner. I

Chapter 2 – A Dynamic Walk

spoke to the landlord for our church building who was a longtime resident of the city and knew many people. I had a brief conversation concerning the old house. "Yes," he exclaimed, "I know the owner of that house, but you are wasting your time. I've already asked about the house for my own use. The owner is not interested in selling, renting, or taking any action on the house." Additionally, he stated, "University officials have inquired about the house and were turned down by the owner." I thanked him for the information and asked him to give me the owner's name and phone number. He seemed to be somewhat irritated with me for being so persistent but he finally relented, giving me the owner's contact information.

I didn't call the owner immediately. I wanted to call because I had now been informed that others were already planning to secure a lease on the house. But I waited. I continued to pray, knowing that my faith was being tested. Numerous times I started to call the owner, but what kept coming to me was "Wait, it's not the right time." This went on for a couple of months, but I kept listening to what I believed God was saying to me. Finally, while in prayer early one morning, I sensed in my spirit a strong impression which said, "Now it's time. Call now about the house." I immediately went to the phone and called the number. I introduced myself to the lady who answered my call and told her of my interest in the house. She politely cut our conversation short by saying, "Pastor, I would be very interested in talking to you about the house, but my mother-in-law, who was the owner of the house, passed away about thirty minutes ago. I am heiress of that property and I will be happy to talk to you about it as soon as we get through this personal loss. You are the first person to call about the house, and I will meet with you soon to discuss these matters."

Chapter 2 – A Dynamic Walk

Only God could have arranged for me to call within thirty minutes after the owner of the house died. If I had called a day earlier, the story may have been totally different. However, the story turned out exactly the way God intended. The new owner rented the property to our church for a very reasonable amount. Through this experience, God had not only answered our prayers, but also taught us the importance of walking in faith.

There are some amazing stories in the Bible that detail the walk of some great men and women of God. These were people who knew their God. One of the most awesome aspects of their story is to understand that their life journey was not limited to their personal experiences, but their stories are incentive for all of us who desire to walk as they did. They became examples for us to follow after. We have the same ability to follow God as did Abraham, Joseph, Deborah, Daniel, Esther, and every other man or woman of God.

Walking in the Spirit
If we live **in the Spirit**, let us also **walk in the Spirit**.
Galatians 5:25

The Scripture admonishes us to make a habit of being guided by the Holy Spirit. That is the key to not living according to our own agenda in life, or according to human nature without God. There is a constant conflict between our human nature and the Holy Spirit. We like to be in control of our life and sometimes find it difficult to yield to God's guidance and instruction in life. As a young man, I took flying lessons. My flight instructor was a strict disciplinarian

Chapter 2 – A Dynamic Walk

whom I had come to appreciate because I was learning to fly well. He once told me that if he ever said he was taking control of the plane, that he would notify me that he was the pilot in command, or PIC. At that point, I was to immediately take my hands off the yoke, thus giving him full control of the aircraft. During one of my lessons, we had just lifted off the runway and climbed to cruise altitude. Suddenly, and with no warning, my instructor informed me that he was Pilot in Command. I immediately took my hands off the controls, and as soon as I had, he took the controls and set the plane in a steep turn. It was so steep that I instinctively reached for the yoke, at which time my instructor rebuked me sharply. "I have the control," he said sternly. He set the plane back to straight and level, returning the control to me, but knowing that I had just learned a valuable lesson. He reminded me that my action could have been detrimental since both of us couldn't be in control at the same time. As tough as it was on me, that lesson was well learned. It wasn't long before I made a spiritual correlation of that lesson. God has given us the freedom to walk out our lives before Him, but there are times He specifically wants us to acknowledge that He is PIC, or in control. Our tendency is to fight for control, especially when it seems like our world is upside down and we feel like we are going down in flames. That's usually when we grab for the control. God does give us freedom but life has proven that we don't always do well being in control, and usually we end up calling on God to pull us out of the steep dive.

If we aren't walking and living in the Spirit, we are walking in the flesh or according to the human nature, without God. What exactly does that mean? When we talk about living in the Spirit, we are defining a walk that is toward the ways of

Chapter 2 – A Dynamic Walk

God. It means to embrace fully His thoughts, His Word, and His will in our lives. Even Jesus prayed, "Not My will, but yours be done." If it was important for Jesus to yield His will, how much more important is it for us? On the other hand, to walk in the flesh means to walk according to our own human understanding and dictates, with or without God's input into our lives. We can't be in the Spirit and in the flesh at the same time. To the extent we are walking according to the dictates of the flesh, we cannot glorify God. The Scripture tells us that no flesh shall glory in His presence, and that there is no good thing in this flesh. (1 Corinthians 1:29) We do have a choice. The right choice for believers is to walk in the Spirit and overcome the fleshly nature which is antagonistic to the Spirit. We need to know what it means to "walk in the Spirit." I believe this to be one of the major messages to New Testament believers. When the Word tells us that to live in the Spirit is to walk in the Spirit, we have a responsibility to do so. It is within our grasp, or else God would not have given us such a mandate. Living in the Spirit is directly related to our walking in the Spirit. As Christians, the only basis for a dynamic walk is when we walk in the Spirit.

The New Testament illustrates what it means to walk in the Spirit through many examples. Obviously, Jesus was the greatest example due to his perfect walk with His heavenly father. He said that the Father had sent Him, and that He always did things that pleased the Father. (John 8:29). Jesus never did anything without His father's approval. Whether He was in the synagogue or the marketplace, Jesus was constantly on a mission. Matthew chapter eight is a good

Chapter 2 – A Dynamic Walk

example of His walk. First, He heals a leper. Leprosy was a dreaded disease known to cause one's flesh to rot. Jews were explicitly instructed on how to deal with the leper. A leper could not travel in public without calling out "unclean" because, by Jewish law, no one was to come close to or touch them. Jesus boldly set out to obey the Father by touching the leper. What an amazing statement Jesus makes when he not only touches the leper, but when He pronounces the leper "cleansed." This healing became a tremendous testimony not only to the priest but to all the people because the leper was "immediately" cleansed.

We see another example of walking in the Spirit when Jesus entered the city of Capernaum, and a Roman soldier came to him to plead with him on behalf of his afflicted servant. The soldier exhibited such great faith that Jesus marveled, saying that He had never seen such faith. Again, Jesus was walking in the spirit, hearing what the Father had to say and spoke what the Father gave Him to speak to the soldier, saying that what you have believed for has been done; go see for yourself. The soldier's servant was healed at that very moment. Jesus then goes on to Peter's house where he saw Peter's mother-in-law sick with a fever. Jesus touched her, the fever left her, and she got up and began to serve others. The same evening Peter's mother-in-law was healed, many sick people were brought to Jesus and He healed all who were sick. Included in that same chapter is the account of Jesus speaking to the wind and waves when a terrifying storm came upon the sea where Jesus and his disciples were crossing in a boat. The disciples were fearful of losing their lives, but Jesus did not condone their unbelief. Instead, He

Chapter 2 – A Dynamic Walk

arose and rebuked the winds and sea and there was a great calm.

I've faced storms that had me fearful of losing my life, and some storms, though not as serious, still presented great challenges to my faith walk. During those times, I've hoped to have the Lord's sympathy or understanding, only to be reminded that He doesn't condone our unbelief. What He questions is, "Where is your faith?" His disciples marveled at the fact that even the wind and waves obeyed Him, but were made keenly aware of their unbelief. I don't believe Jesus was condemning them for unbelief, but exhorting them, or prompting them toward a greater walk in the Spirit. These accounts are only a few that represent what it means to walk like Jesus walked. However, His walk involved much more than performing miracles. Jesus came to earth preaching and teaching a new message. In Matthew chapter five we read The Beatitudes, which were foundational to His Kingdom message. In that message, Jesus began the discourse saying, "Blessed are the poor in spirit, for theirs is the kingdom of heaven." (v3) He addressed those who mourn, the meek, those who hunger and thirst for righteousness, the merciful, those who are pure in heart, the peacemakers, and lastly those persecuted for righteousness sake. (v's 5-10) He emphasized that "theirs is the kingdom of heaven." He then launched into teachings that challenged religious tradition. He used terminology like, "You have heard," but "I tell you." Jesus brought with Him a paradigm shift. This was a shift that would shape the New Testament church which was to be built upon the foundation that He was laying.

Chapter 2 – A Dynamic Walk

Walking in the Spirit is *maintaining a God consciousness*, or an awareness to His leading and guiding presence *at all times*, and obeying His promptings. God has defined and provided a path for His people to "walk in His ways." Walking in the spirit can also be expressed as keeping in step with the Spirit. When we keep in step with someone, we are imitating or following them closely. When we are talking about keeping in step with God's Spirit, we will listen to and obey what He is saying. We will also learn what God's Word says so that we are sure we are hearing clearly God's voice. (Psalm 119:11) The Holy Spirit will never do anything contrary to the Bible, the Word of God. If we hear something that does not line up with God's Word, we will know we are not hearing God's voice.

The Bible speaks of a "path of righteousness," and, the steps of a good man being ordered by the Lord. There was a time when many Christians wore bracelets with the acronym WWJD (What Would Jesus Do). That was a form of an awareness of God's presence, and many people attested to how much that awareness had influenced their thoughts and behavior in practical ways.

During one period of my life, I began each day with earnest prayer that God would help me walk in the path that He had already planned for me. I set out to follow the leading of the Holy Spirit each day, my faith was ignited by a Scripture verse (Ephesians 2:10) which says, God has already prepared a plan for us to walk in. Then one morning, the Holy Spirit spoke to me, not in an audible voice, but with an impression of something He wanted me to do. I was impressed to go to

Chapter 2 – A Dynamic Walk

a place of business that I knew to be owned by a wealthy individual who was known for losing his temper. I sensed that God wanted me to speak to him, but I was not told what to say. I did not know the man personally, but was very aware of his poor reputation. My first response to this impression was to question the Lord out loud saying, "Lord, is that really you? I don't know this man personally and can't be sure that I can even get on his property to talk to him." I received what I believed was a word from God, saying, "You have been asking to walk with me on a daily basis. Are you willing to follow My guidance?" At that point I got into my car and drove across town to the man's place of business. Once inside the building, I met the man's secretary and introduced myself. I asked her if her boss was available. She informed me that he was not in at the moment and wasn't sure when he would return. I was relieved because I thought I was off the hook, but the Lord had other plans.

As I headed back to my vehicle, the Holy Spirit prompted me again in my spirit saying, "I haven't released you to leave. You are to wait here until he returns." In my immaturity, I replied, "Okay, Lord! I will wait here for ten minutes. If you want me to speak to this man, I need you to have him come to me because I don't even know what he looks like." I checked my watch to be sure the Lord knew how serious I was. Moments went by and nobody entered the building. Seven minutes later, a well-dressed man walked into the building and straight down the corridor to where I was standing. He introduced himself and asked me who I was. I looked him straight in the eye and told him my name and I told him that I was a minister of the Gospel. I said I was

Chapter 2 – A Dynamic Walk

there because the Lord had given me a word to speak to him. He motioned for me to follow him to his office. As we entered his executive office, I had a mixed sense of awe and wonder at God's leading me. He sat down behind his large teakwood desk and asked me to please speak. I rose from my chair, pointed my finger directly at his face and began to speak words that surprised even me. Remembering his reputation for having a bad temper, I thought he might throw me out of his office at any moment. When I was finished delivering the word God gave me, the man got out of his oversized leather chair and knelt on the floor of his office, right in front of picture windows. For the next few minutes, it seemed as though everything stood still. There were no phones ringing, nobody knocking on the door of his office, and no other distractions of any kind. He asked me to pray with him to receive Jesus as his savior, and in one of the most extraordinary moments in either of our lives, Jesus came into this man's life.

The miraculous events that led up to the moment that this man gave his life to Jesus helped me see the marvelous things God can do when we keep in step with the Holy Spirit. There were other miracles that followed in the life of this man and his family. The last time I saw him before he went home to be with Jesus, we attended the same prayer meeting, unaware that the other was there. I noticed that he was sitting on the front row praying and worshipping God. As the meeting finished, he turned to leave and as he did, we made eye contact. He came to me, embraced me with tears in his eyes, and began to thank me for "never giving up" on him. He went on to tell me how the peace of God had filled his life

Chapter 2 – A Dynamic Walk

and how he was no longer controlled by anger and hatred toward others. I could see the visible peace of God in his countenance. It wasn't long after that meeting until he passed into Heaven, but he did not do so without leaving a beautiful testimony of the Lord's mercy, grace, and goodness. I remain grateful that one day, many years before, I had obeyed a prompting of the Holy Spirit, and as a result, a wayward businessman came to a peace with God, and was now in Heaven.

Chapter 3 – Prayer Dynamics

Chapter 3

Prayer Dynamics

> "There is no one who calls on Your name,
> Who awakens and causes himself to take hold of You…"
> (Isaiah 64:7 AMP)

Have you ever had a time when you questioned the usefulness of prayer? Perhaps you've had thoughts of whether God even hears your prayers. Most people who believe in God know they should pray. However, there often seems to be a lack of motivation, time, or desire to pray. One Scripture that inspires faith states "…The earnest (heartfelt, continued) prayer of a righteous man makes tremendous power available – dynamic in its working." (James 5:16, Amplified Bible). An account goes on to detail how Elijah was a man, just like us. He prayed that it not rain for three and one-half years and it did not rain. When God directed him, he prayed again that it would rain, and the rains came. That is an impressive account of the power of prayer and the Scripture says that it's available to a righteous person. This Scripture applies to all who have been made righteous by the blood of Jesus. We are the righteousness of God in Christ

Chapter 3 – Prayer Dynamics

Jesus. That means when we pray, we can, and should, expect God's results. God can and will invade our prayer lives if we ask Him to do so. If we, like His disciples, ask Him to "teach us to pray."

I married my high school sweetheart. She was the daughter of a minister and had a strong spiritual foundation of which a key component was prayer. Even before we were married, she was challenging and inspiring me to a greater, more meaningful prayer life. One of my first experiences with God answering prayer for me, where I had no doubt that He answered, occurred while I was home on furlough. I had developed a very severe cough and respiratory condition just before coming home on leave. In one of my coughing fits during the night, Ruth asked me if she could pray for me. She prayed a quiet prayer asking God to relieve me of the terrible coughing. I made one more little hacking cough, and the cough stopped. I was healed, and I was utterly amazed. There is nothing dynamic about unanswered prayer. Because effective praying is not based on mere feeling, we must have faith that our prayers are heard and answered. Answered prayer is dynamic. Answered prayer becomes the fabric of personal testimony that brings glory to God. When God answers our prayers, we are encouraged, give thanks to the Lord, and grow in faith, and as you share your experiences with others, it helps inspire faith in them. It is important to note that God does not always answer our prayers in ways we expect, nor necessarily when we expect, but having the assurance that He has heard your prayer and knowing that He will answer not only strengthens your faith and testimony, but inspires others as well.

Chapter 3 – Prayer Dynamics

Praying and Abiding

Jesus said that if we maintain a dedicated, constant walk with Him, we can pray knowing that what we've asked will be done for us. (John 14:13) That is a powerful incentive to pray. If we believe what Jesus said, our faith will increase greatly for our prayers to be answered. The conditions which we must meet is a life of abiding or living in Him, with His words living in us. (Psalm 119:11; John 15:7) If we are living so close to Jesus that we can feel His heartbeat and know Him and His desires, then our prayers will become what He desires. (Psalm 37:4) If His words are living or abiding in us and are so much a part of us that they become the way we think or act, then we can ask what we desire and receive those answers to our prayers.

Praying in the Will of God

Dynamic prayer is centered in the will of God. The Scripture tells us that our confidence in the Lord assures us that if we ask according to His will, that He hears us. That is a powerful statement! But even more powerful is that if He hears us, He answers us and gives us our request. (1 John 5:14-15) The condition is to ask according to His will. That is dynamic and that will boost your trust in Him.

Keys to Prayer

Over the course of many years of ministry, one of my favorite topics to teach is on the subject of prayer. When Jesus's disciples asked that He teach them to pray (Luke 11:1), He responded by giving them several keys to effective prayer. When we understand prayer as a form of communication with our Heavenly Father on an intimate

Chapter 3 – Prayer Dynamics

level, we realize that prayer is also a relational aspect of our fellowship with God. He is my Father and thus I need to know His will, His ways, His heart, His Word, and His wisdom in order to pray accurately. The scripture teaches us that if we pray according to His will, He hears us, and further, if He hears us, then we know we can expect answers to our prayers. (I John 5:14)

As I was teaching this, I was reminded of my father. Even as a child, I knew my dad to be a person of his word. When I was nine years old, I told my father that I wanted a 22-caliber rifle. He told me that he felt I was too young at the time, but that he would get me a rifle when I was twelve years old. I did not doubt that I was going to get a rifle. I told all my friends, "I'm going to get a rifle when I turn twelve years old." On my twelfth birthday, I was handed a gift in a long box. Before I could even get the wrapping off, I was super excited because I just knew that it was a rifle. Why? Because my father had told me several years before that he would get me a rifle on my twelfth birthday. What that did for me was validate my dad's integrity. He was a man with character. Integrity was a prominent characteristic of his, and because of that, he could be trusted. It was his integrity that assured me that I was going to get that rifle. I never doubted his word to me. As I pondered these things, I realized that I had seen a reflection of my Heavenly Father being lived out through my father.

My earthly father became a reflection to me of my Heavenly Father, which caused me to think of God's integrity, righteousness, and holiness, as well as His faithfulness and love. There are many more attributes of God which define who He is. What He says He will do, He will do. God is the same, always. He is constant in His nature and His will for man. Therefore, when I pray according to His will, my faith for answered prayer rests in the trust of who He is. He never acts outside of His sovereign will. (Numbers 23:19; Hebrews 13:8; James 1:17)

Prayer and Righteousness
In Genesis chapter eighteen we read of how Abraham prayed. Abrahams's nephew, Lot, had taken his family to Sodom to live. Sodom was known as an ultra-wicked place. The Lord had shown Abraham the judgement that was coming on these wicked cities. Abraham, concerned not only for his family, but for any other righteous people, boldly made an appeal to God. In verse 23 Abraham asks, "Will you sweep away the righteous with the wicked?" Abraham goes on to appeal to the Lord by asking, "Suppose there are fifty righteous?" Unrelenting, Abraham continues to intercede with righteous God on behalf of people, hoping that the city can be spared by righteous people. He persistently pleads with the Lord and asked if He would spare the city for forty-five righteous; forty, thirty, twenty, and ultimately ten, and finally God says, "I will not destroy it for ten."

Abraham's faith seemed rooted in the will of God and he prayed accordingly. We as believers are taught that we can also pray, as did Jesus, "…not my will, but yours be done." (Luke 22:42)

Chapter 3 – Prayer Dynamics

Our faith is released as the assurance of knowing that we are praying according to His will is settled in our heart. We know that He is righteous: "The Lord is righteous in all His ways…" (Psalm 145:17, NKJV).

God's Holiness
God's holiness is descriptive of His divinity as it is manifested through His justice, purity of character, and power. It also denotes a distinction between the creature and the Creator.

The Bible often refers to God's name as holy. The Scripture states that His name is awesome and holy. We are admonished to "Glory in His holy name" (Psalm 105:3). God wants us to know that He is holy and that He has made way for us to enter His holy presence. This entrance is possible because of the redemptive graces made available to us by Jesus. (Hebrews 4:15-16) It is because of Him that we can confidently enter into God's holy presence. According to the Bible, by the blood of Jesus we have been cleansed of all unrighteousness that would prevent us from being in His holy presence. (Hebrews 10:10; 1 John 1:7) We now have every right to appeal to God by His holy character. We become holy people calling on Holy God who desires to bring glory and honor to His Holy name through us.

There are times when we need to take a hard look at our life if prayers are unanswered. We are often quick to blame "the enemy" for hindering God's answers to our prayers, until God begins to reveal that He wants to deal with us. He deals with us on issues such as disobedience, unbelief, not

Chapter 3 – Prayer Dynamics

forgiving others, and broken relationships. Unanswered prayer does not mean that God has not made a promise or that He doesn't care what we are going through, but it may be because He wants us to bring glory and honor to His name in all we do. (Colossians 3:17,23; 1 Corinthians 10:31) We must get sin out of our lives if we are going on with Holy God!

An example of this is found in the book of Joshua, chapter seven. Following close on the heels of the conquest of Jericho, where the Israelites had seen first-hand the mighty walls of Jericho come crashing to the ground, the Israelites find themselves facing the less formidable city of Ai. Compared to Jericho, this should have been an easy victory. Just after Moses's death, God had given Joshua promises, telling him that he would possess the land his feet walked on. Further, he reassured him that He would be with him, just as He had been with Moses. Having these promises, Joshua led God's people forward in faith, knowing God's promises were good.

Now, at what should have been an easy victory, the Israelites suffer humiliation and defeat at the hands of their enemy. Joshua was stunned! His powerful army, backed by all the promises of God, was defeated by the army at Ai. What humiliation! And now his people lost heart. Joshua, the great leader of God's people, falls on his face in God's presence and calls on God. I can only imagine what that prayer meeting was like. Surely, Joshua was reminding the Lord of His promises. After all, God had promised him victory in battle. He poured out his heart to God, by asking God things

Chapter 3 – Prayer Dynamics

like, why did You even bring us over the Jordan? Was it just to have the Amorites destroy us? But out of his anguish, Joshua asks the one question that appealed to God's character when He asked, "...And what wilt thou do unto thy great name?" (Joshua 7:9). God answers Joshua in keeping with His holy character by telling him that the people have sinned and transgressed His covenant by stealing and hiding an "accursed" thing among their stuff. Further, He declared that it was for this reason that the children of Israel could not stand before their enemies, and in fact, had turned their backs before their enemies. This was so serious that God told Joshua that He would not be with him anymore if he did not deal with the sin issue. God was saying that there was no default on His word, but that the sin hidden in the camp through a man named Achan would prevent God from keeping His covenant word to them. God told Joshua to get up off his face, stop questioning Him and instructed him to get the sin out of the camp. Joshua followed God's instructions, and once again, victory came to the Israelites.

God has made great and wonderful promises, covenant promises to His people today. At times, we find ourselves struggling with defeat. We know God's word is true; we know what Jesus did for us, and yet we sometimes stumble. Like Joshua, I've found myself on my face crying out to God because of defeat, unanswered prayer, and ultimate discouragement. It was at one of those moments that God revealed the power of the account in Joshua to me. He spoke to my heart, revealed to me an area of the sin of unbelief that I was hiding in my camp. And, as He spoke to Joshua, I felt admonished to get up off my face, break the fast I was on, repent for unbelief, and begin giving thanks to the Lord for His victory. Just as He did with Joshua, God once again honored His word to me and brought me victory over my spiritual enemy.

If you are struggling with areas of defeat in your Christian walk, perhaps you can be encouraged to ask God if there is any sin in your camp. Trust Him to reveal anything to you that is hindering your intimate fellowship or relationship with Him. He has promised you that if you will confess your sin, He is faithful and just to forgive you, to remove your sin from you as far as the east is from the west, to cast them into a sea of forgetfulness, never to be remembered against you again. (1 John 1:9; Psalm 103:12; Micah 7:19) Don't give in to discouragement and despair. (Joshua 1:9) Rid your camp of sin. Arise! God is waiting to lead you into a path of victory and bring honor to His Name through you.

God's Sovereignty
The sovereignty of God speaks of his absolute dominion, supremacy, or power. The Bible states that God rules over all the earth. (Psalm 22:28, 103:19) He not only created the heavens and the earth, He rules His creation.

King Jehoshaphat trusted in God's sovereignty. Jehoshaphat was facing a massive assault in Judah by the collective armies of Moab and Ammon, along with others. According to this account, Jehoshaphat feared and set himself to seek the Lord. He appealed in prayer asking for help saying, "O Lord God of our fathers, are You not God in heaven, and do You

Chapter 3 – Prayer Dynamics

not rule over all the kingdoms of the nations, and in Your hand is there not power and might, so that no one is able to withstand You?" (2 Chronicles 20:6) Jehoshaphat had a lot at stake. He could either trust in God's sovereignty, believing that God was in control, or he could choose to take another path. He made a wise choice by leading all the people to trust in the Lord. Learning to trust in God's sovereignty while not depending on our own understanding requires faith.

Years ago, while pastoring a church in Texas, I was scheduled to leave for a ministry trip to another state. While finishing packing my belongings for the week-long trip, several unexpected delays occurred and all the last-minute details were taking longer than usual. Growing somewhat frustrated, and concerned that I might miss my flight, I began to express my irritations out loud. My wife sweetly smiled and attempted to assure me that everything would be alright. Well, as so often happens when I am in a hurry, I got behind some slow-moving traffic on the way to the airport, and the clock was ever moving toward my departure time. When it looked as though there was no way I could get to the gate on time, I once again blurted out my frustration, even to the point of raising my voice in anger. My wife reminded me of the fact that God was sovereign; in other words, He is in control. She continued, "You need to trust Him. If you are supposed to be there, you will; and if not, you don't need to go." I knew she was right, and I immediately repented for my poor attitude and began, instead, to declare my trust in God, knowing that He knew exactly when and where I needed to be. I was trusting in God's sovereignty. God's peace came to me at that moment.

Chapter 3 – Prayer Dynamics

I hurried to the gate to board the plane and realized that I was the last person to board. Moving on through the first-class section to coach where my assigned seat was, I noticed a gentleman also moving toward the rear of the plane. A flight attendant approached both of us and said "Gentlemen, I'm sorry to inform you that the coach section is full; there are no available seats." Before I had time to react, she smiled sweetly and said, "I'm afraid you gentlemen will have to ride in first-class, and there is no additional charge to you." As you might imagine, I was feeling a twinge of guilt over having had such an untrusting attitude earlier. But my faith was sure in high gear now, and I could hardly wait to call my wife and tell her how "spot-on" she had been with her encouragement to trust in the Lord's will with this trip. The other man and I took the last two seats on this flight. Our seats were next to each other; so it was easy to strike up a conversation about our good fortune.

He asked me what I did for a living, and I replied that I was a pastor. He informed me that he worked for a large media organization and was on a business trip. He also had been running late getting to the airport. After a few minutes of small talk, he asked, "Since you are a minister, is it okay if I share something personal with you?" I assured him that would be okay. I was thinking how good it was of the Lord to give me an opportunity to minister to somebody after I had repented of my poor attitude. He began to share with me the fact that he was having marital problems. Ultimately, he confided that his marriage was at a crossroad and that without something miraculous happening, he did not think it would survive. I had just recently been counseling with a

Chapter 3 – Prayer Dynamics

married couple who were having some of the same issues. Through counseling and prayer, we had seen God restore their marriage. I began sharing a little of their story with this total stranger because it was a fresh testimony of God's divine intervention and reconciliation of two people in a failing marriage. I thought this testimony would be an encouragement to my seatmate. I accidentally did something during my sharing that I had never done before. I let the first names of the two individuals whose testimony I was referring to slip out of my mouth. I hurriedly moved on in the conversation hoping that he had not heard the names and that the emphasis was on their testimony, not who they were. As I continued, I noticed tears welling up in his eyes and soon streaming down his cheek. I thought to myself, "Wow, Lord, you are getting through to this guy!" Finally, placing his hand on my shoulder, he said, "Stop. I've got to tell you something!" As I ceased talking, he looked me straight in the eye and said, "Did you say the lady whose name you ministered to was Lynn?" I said, "Yes." He said, with tears now freely flowing, "Lynn is my ex-wife. I have lost contact with her over the years. Neither of us were Christians when we were married, but I have since remarried and became a Christian several years ago. I've prayed for Lynn often and asked the Lord if He would just please let me know that she was OK spiritually, hoping that she was now a Christian." I was now utterly speechless. What are the odds of two strangers coming together like we did, I wondered, and then to have such amazing things happen as we shared with one another. One could not have planned this incident and been able to carry it out. Only God in His

Chapter 3 – Prayer Dynamics

sovereign will could do such a thing. God intervenes in our lives by His sovereign will, and when He does, it is dynamic and can change the course of lives and history.

Have you ever experienced times when you didn't understand why things were happening as they were, or the circumstances of your life had spiraled out of control, and perhaps you even despaired of life itself? Maybe you've wondered where God was when you needed Him most. Maybe the Christians with whom you shared didn't seem to understand and their well- intentioned words were meaningless religious rhetoric. Bible stories were just that – stories. Inspiring, yet seemingly out of reach for you. In times like this, ask God to give you a revelation of His sovereignty. The Bible says to cast our cares on Him, trust Him, and acknowledge Him in all our ways. (1 Peter 5:7; Proverbs 3:5-6)

The Book of Daniel contains a couple of the best testimonies to illustrate the dynamic of God's sovereignty. The first tells of three Hebrew men; Shadrach, Meshach, and Abednego.

These men were peers of Daniel. They loved God and were men of great conviction. They refused to honor the King's decree to bow down in worship before a golden image that he had set up. The three were given opportunity to recant their position, but chose rather to stand true to their conviction. As a result of their decision not to bow down, they were sentenced to be placed in a fiery furnace. At their sentencing, their trust in the sovereignty of God was clearly demonstrated in their reply to the King. They told the King

Chapter 3 – Prayer Dynamics

that God was able to deliver them from the fiery furnace, and, that if He didn't deliver them, they still would refuse to bow down to the golden image. By their declaration they stated their trust in the absolute sovereignty of God in their lives. The final result was that God miraculously delivered the three, and the King, in a dramatic reversal from the death sentence, promoted the three men in Babylon.

Another testimony of God's sovereignty is that of Daniel. He was a godly man who possessed great wisdom, was an interpreter of dreams, and who had favor with both God and man. He was elevated to the highest position of authority in Babylon, with only the King himself having more authority. Daniel's life was consecrated to the God he served, and by all accounts, he was a man of resolute conviction. Refusing to obey the King's edict that he was not allowed to petition any man or god but the King for thirty days, Daniel chose rather to pray to and worship the one true God. It was due to his refusal to violate his convictions that he ended up being cast into a den of lions. He trusted implicitly in the sovereignty of God. King Darius, who had placed Daniel in the den of lions, was fond of Daniel, but expressed his trust that God could deliver Daniel. Ultimately, Daniel was able to declare that God had shut the mouths of hungry lions to spare him. His trust in the sovereignty of God was tested. Daniel passed the test.

Chapter 3 – Prayer Dynamics

Persistent Prayer

A genuine meaning of prayer is that we get a hold on God,
not just an answer.
(unknown)

Persistent prayers are dynamic and can be described as the ability to "press-on, at all costs," or to remain steadfast and resolute. Prayer is one of the essential dynamics available to believers. Jesus spoke a parable regarding prayer recorded in Luke 18:1 which states that we should always pray and never give up. He then conveyed the parable of the persistent widow appealing to an unjust judge. The judge was so frustrated with her persistence that he finally determined he had to vindicate her because she was wearing him out. Jesus then went on to say that the judge would eventually make a judgement, just to stop the widow from pestering him. Her persistence paid off. There is a story in the Old Testament Book of Daniel which also points out the importance of persistence. Daniel had been fasting and praying for twenty-one days. After these days of prayer, the Angel Gabriel appeared to him and informed him that his prayers had been heard from the beginning. Jesus taught that men should always pray and never give up. If we must pray twenty-one days like Daniel did to get answers from God, or perhaps even longer, will we continue to pray until we have the assurance our prayers have been answered? Answers to our prayers may be closer than we know. I was told a humorous anecdote once that illustrates my point. It told of a person who swam three-fourths of the way across the English Channel, and got tired, so he turned around and went back home. It is not funny however, when we have prayed for

Chapter 3 – Prayer Dynamics

such a long time, that we grow weary and give up. How many people living for God today do so because of someone else's persistent prayers? One of the greatest blessings to me is that of having parents and a wife who learned the importance of persistent prayer. At one time in my life I had strayed from the Lord, but as a result of the persistent prayers of my wife and my mother, God restored me to walking a right path. The Bible, referencing Isaiah's concern for a rebellious people, states that none of those people were stirring themselves up, calling on the Lord, or taking hold of the Lord. (Isaiah 64:7). It seems the message here is to stir ourselves to pray until we know we have come to terms with the Lord in answer to our prayers.

Persistence in prayer became a reality to me not long after I started attending a small Bible College in Florida. For over a year before enrolling in Bible College, I had a cyst develop just above and to the outside of my left eye. In the church I was attending, the pastor taught that God still heals people today. A friend then pointed me to a Scripture and shared with me the importance of the words "were healed" as used in that Scripture verse. He informed me that the verb form was in the past tense. In other words, this was an already accomplished action. I had not known much about divine healing, but my faith to believe for healing was being stirred. I had the conviction that if I was going to preach the Gospel, it had to be the whole Gospel and therefore had to work for me, or I did not intend to teach it to anybody else. Months went by, and the cyst continued to grow larger. By the time I had arrived in Florida to attend Bible College, the cyst was as large as a small egg. It was unsightly, and I was

Chapter 3 – Prayer Dynamics

embarrassed to be in public. By now, however, I was tenacious in holding to the Word of God, which said I was healed even though the cyst was still on my face. Several people chided me asking, "Why don't you go get a doctor to remove that thing from your head?" My answer was always the same, and I remained steadfast in my faith. "God has healed me" I would say, "And I don't know when, but the time will come when that cyst will go from my body by the power of God." My faith was being tested but was growing, as was my prayer life as a result of the classes I was taking at the college. One of those courses was on Divine Healing.

Several months after having begun attending Bible classes at the college, my pastor, who was also President of the Bible College, asked me to speak at a Wednesday night service at the Church. As I stood before the congregation that evening, the first statement I made was about the cyst, large and visible for all to see. I told the people that even though there was no manifestation of healing in my body, I knew God was faithful to His word and that the cyst had to go. "I don't know when, but it must go" I boldly declared. "You will see, and you will know that God has done it." I told them that faith does not work according to man's schedule, but that faith is always in the "now," taken from Hebrews 11:1 which states "Now faith is the substance of things hoped for, the evidence of things not seen." I knew in my heart that my faith had more substance than the cyst and that my healing was by faith which represented evidence not yet seen.

Chapter 3 – Prayer Dynamics

One Sunday morning church service, my wife and I went home to have lunch and rest before the evening service. Suddenly, my wife looked me eye to eye and asked me whether or not I believed God could heal me. Did I believe God can heal such a thing? Her pointed questions sent my thoughts into a whirl. I tried to muster up all the faith I had to answer her questions, and finally got the words out, "Yes, I believe He can." I thought maybe that would satisfy her. What I didn't know was that God was using her to nudge me toward a miracle. Then she fired the final question at me by asking, "Do you believe God will take that cyst off your head before the church service this evening?" That question hit me like a tidal wave. I had been praying for God to remove this growth for a long time. Now, in a moment of time, my faith was challenged. I calmly responded to my wife, "Yes, I believe God will do that," but inwardly, I was fighting the fight of faith. Seeing my struggle, my wife said: "Why don't you go rest, God is doing this." I agreed to lie down, but rather than go to sleep I began to pray. I said, "Lord, even as Jonah was spit out of that fish because he was contrary to that fish's system, I am asking that my body reject this cyst because it runs counter to your will for my body." I suddenly had the urge to stand in front of our bathroom mirror, look at that cyst, and declare out loud that it had to leave my body in the name of Jesus. As I stood looking at the cyst, I placed my hand on it and began my declaration. God honored my prayers that day and the first miracle for me to see personally was in my body. The cyst popped off my head into the bathroom lavatory sink. I shouted "Hallelujah, glory to God!" so loudly that my wife was startled. I hurriedly went to my wife and upon looking at my head, she began to shout

Chapter 3 – Prayer Dynamics

praises to God as well. Ecstatic doesn't seem adequate to describe what I felt at that moment. Unbridled joy, praise, and thanks to the Lord came from deep in my heart.

I could hardly wait to walk into the church service that evening. As we walked into the sanctuary, I saw people begin to stare at me, whispers started going throughout the sanctuary and people began to praise and worship God. I could hear people gasping in awe, and some fell to their knees. A miracle had taken place, and they had all just become witnesses to God's faithfulness and goodness. I was at church that morning with a growth on my head, and now, that same day, it was gone! One former skeptic said to me, "I always knew God could take that thing off your head." Undaunted, I just smiled, gave thanks to the Lord, and most importantly rejoiced at the beautiful thing God had done for me. Now I had experienced the God who heals. Through several years of persistent prayer, God had revealed Himself to me and many others as the God of miracles, signs, and wonders.

Word of this miracle quickly spread around different parts of the United States. Several years later, people upon meeting me were still commenting in amazement at what God had done for me. Where once had been a large growth, now remained only a small scar.

Consistent Prayer

Consistent means to do something the same way over time. It can also mean to be in agreement with something. The Bible indicates that Jesus prayed in the early morning as a

Chapter 3 – Prayer Dynamics

habit. Some of the people who have had the most influence in my life are those who are consistent in their prayer habits.

The Scripture records in the book of Acts an account of what many today have termed, "the early church," or the "New Testament Church." In other words, this was the first record of the church that came into existence after the death, burial, and resurrection of Jesus; this became the foundation of the church of which the Lord Jesus had spoken. This church was ignited by the power of the cross, His shed blood, and the power of the Holy Spirit. There were several key factors that contributed to the success of the Church. The people of the church adhered to the doctrines of the Church as taught to them by the apostles, they maintained fellowship and communion, and the Scripture states that they "continued steadfastly" in prayer. (Acts 2:42) It was a church given to consistent prayer, and as a result of their prayers, this was a church filled with the Spirit, a fearless church, and an influential church. Reading through the Book of Acts, it is safe to say that the New Testament Church was indeed an influential church. It possessed the energy, force, and motion to qualify as dynamic. The church was a revolutionary, world-changing faith community, infused with the power and gifts of the Holy Spirit. The Early Church did not become a dynamic entity without strong faith and consistent praying.

I once had the privilege of meeting with the President of a Latin American nation. In our conversation, he conveyed to me the importance of consistency in prayer. His predecessors had not been Christian believers, and as revival

Chapter 3 – Prayer Dynamics

swept across the nation, more and more evangelical Christians began to pray that God would bless their country with a Christian president. He went on to tell me that he and many of the believers felt that he was the answer to the prayers for a Christian president. He said that once he was in power, the people stopped praying with the same fervency for their country. Consequently, it wasn't long before this Christian president was toppled from power. Evangelicals readily admitted their mistake and began praying fervently again, and God did respond to their prayers and once again gave them several influential Christians within their national government. It was a good reminder to be steadfast in prayers knowing that what is birthed in prayer must be sustained by prayer.

Commitment to Prayer

Prayer doesn't always come easy. Have you ever noticed times when you could find the time to do just about anything but pray? Have you had times when you made a fresh commitment to pray only to be bombarded with every imaginable distraction such as ringing doorbells, barking dogs, crying babies, unplanned phone calls and myriads of other distractions? One of the more common distractions for many is what I call a "wandering mind syndrome." That is when one gets all settled and ready for prayer, and suddenly their mind wanders off in many directions. It could be something as simple as tasks needing to be completed around the house to something as serious as the family or work relationships, but the point is a wandering mind prevents one from being focused in prayer. Most people live their lives on a tight schedule, and difficulty in being focused

Chapter 3 – Prayer Dynamics

in prayer becomes discouraging. It takes time and commitment to get focused.

I've often thought about all the distractions believers in the early church faced. Many were being persecuted, severely tested, imprisoned, and even martyred for their faith. It seems that the people of the early church had one of two choices. They could either make a firm commitment to prayer or they could become disillusioned and discouraged to the point that their prayer life became ineffective.

The Bible conveys so much about the church in the Book of Acts. Early in the book, it is noted that, "These all *continued with one accord in prayer and supplication...*" Acts 1:13-14. The word 'continued' as used here is defined in the Greek as proskartereo; to persevere in a thing, to adhere to firmly, and to be in close pursuit or intent upon.

I recently read an account of a well-noted man of prayer which illustrates the importance of perseverance in prayer. One day this man began praying for several of his friends to come to salvation. After many months, one of them came to the Lord. Several years later, others were converted. The man persevered in prayer for the remainder of his friends. He never gave up believing that they would accept Christ! Ultimately, his faith and perseverance came to fruition when all those he had been praying for came to salvation.

Soon after I began attending Bible College, new teachings stirred my Spirit to know God in ways that I had never dreamed possible. One of those stirrings was in the area of

Chapter 3 – Prayer Dynamics

praying prayers that got results. I was inspired to pray and not give up. I soon discovered that commitment to prayer usually doesn't come about without a trying of one's faith. My first experience with this level of committed prayer came soon after I began attending the college. We had just moved to Pensacola, Florida. Our daughter, who was our firstborn child, was less than one year old, and I had no job when we first arrived. The move had taken not only every bit of faith I had, but in the process of moving, we had exhausted our available finances. An unusually cold winter was upon us. We had moved into a small mobile home that was cold and drafty. We were happy though, because we knew we were in the will of God.

I was already taking classes at the college and my faith was being challenged, but it was growing. Each answered prayer served to make me want to pray more. It was during this time that I earnestly kept our financial needs in prayer. Each prayer experience seemed to bring me to a new level, each testing my faith. I prayed earnestly for our finances for several days, and I finally received an assurance that God had not only heard my prayers, but that I could now hold fast to a promise that my prayers were answered. Previously, I was of the mindset of, "I will believe it when I see it." Now, I was being challenged to "believe it before I could see it." Two Scripture verses came to mind at the time. One was Colossians 4:2 which states, "Continue in prayer, and watch in the same with thanksgiving." I believed that I had been constant in prayer and now I was at the point of giving thanks. I learned that there were prayers of petition, prayers of praise, spiritual warfare prayers, and prayers of

Chapter 3 – Prayer Dynamics

thanksgiving. I believed that I was now well armed with Scripture to fight the fight of faith and I was committed to praying, expecting to get results. This is in keeping with Jesus' teaching, which says that when you pray, believe. (Matthew 21:22)

Since I had an assurance that my prayers were answered, I began to thank the Lord for meeting a specific dollar amount. I knew I was stretching my faith. I was going to believe God for the answer, without saying anything to anyone but my wife. I continued to thank the Lord for several days, not knowing how, or when, but still knowing that God had already answered my prayers. The deadline for the financial need I had was quickly approaching, which kept me even more earnest in my thanksgiving to the Lord for meeting this need. Finally, the day before my deadline for this financial need, I felt the need to stand in the yard and watch for the mail delivery. I had told my wife that we were going to get a check in the mail that day. We lived on a small lane, which was a dead-end. The mailman would always make his way down the lane, delivering mail on one side, reach the end of the lane, and start back up the other side of the lane delivering mail. So I stood and waited. As he approached my mailbox, I inched closer, hardly able to contain myself. As though I were not even there, the mailman passed right on by me, not even slowing down. I was incredulous. I turned to my wife and said, "He forgot to give me our mail!" She had believed with me for a miracle, and even then she stood with me, encouraging me, even when it looked as if there was no mail for us that day. I watched as the mailman went all the way to the end of the

Chapter 3 – Prayer Dynamics

lane and up the opposite side, passing us by again. I kept telling my wife, "He has our mail! He forgot to give us our mail!" Just before he reached the end of the lane at the entrance to the park, he stopped to talk to the manager of the park who happened to be waiting for him. I noticed that the manager was pointing in my direction, and in my heart, I knew that he had my mail. Suddenly, he turned around and came my direction. When he got to me, he stopped, pulled out a piece of mail, and stuck it out the door of his mail-wagon. It was for us!! With no explanation of why he had passed me by, he handed me the only piece of mail we got that day, and he drove off.

I was beyond elated. I hastily opened the envelope, and there, in the mail, was a check for the amount I needed. Not only had God performed a miracle for us by meeting the financial obligation, but He also proved His faithfulness to us personally. I learned a lesson through that experience that continues with me all these years later, and that is that our Heavenly Father will honor our persistence in prayer if we will pray and not give up.

Communion in Prayer
Communion is defined as the sharing or exchanging of intimate thoughts and feelings, especially when the exchange is on a mental or spiritual level. Since communion is a sharing of intimate thoughts and feelings, prayer could be defined as an informal exchange with God. In that context, prayer is a form of communion. Jesus taught such through His teachings and, more importantly, by example. The Scripture indicates that Jesus was in constant communion with the

Chapter 3 – Prayer Dynamics

Father. We know that Jesus prayed often and effectually. At the tomb of Lazarus, he thanked His Father for always hearing him and said, "I know that you always hear me." (John 11:42) Jesus said He did nothing but what the Father told Him and that He always did those things that pleased the Father. (John 5:19, 8:29) He would not have been able to make such bold declarations had He not been in constant communion with the Father.

Influence of Prayer
Prayer is one of the most dynamic influences known. Merriam Webster Dictionary defines influence as "The power to change or affect someone or something: the power to cause changes without directly forcing them to happen."

The Bible is full of examples of men and women praying in faith. Their prayers influenced Kings, changed nations, moved the heart of God, and influenced the known world through supernatural results.

A tremendous exhortation and example of this kind of prayer is found in the New Testament. The Scripture tells us that fervent, consistent prayers of believers make tremendous power available, and goes on to say that this intense form of prayer is dynamic. (James 5:16, AMP) We are talking about dynamic prayer: prayer that gets results and that has influence wherever it is directed. Elijah prayed that it not rain for three and one-half years, and it did not rain. He then prayed for rain, and the rains came. The effective prayer he prayed had an influence on all those around him. We can pray with the same power and influence. Our

Chapter 3 – Prayer Dynamics

prayers, like Elijah's, can be effective enough to change the world around us. Many believe that it is possible and dare to step out in faith. There are those who have determined that God wants to hear and answer prayer. They are weary of empty, religious, shallow praying. Many of those prayers are faithless and without any positive influence. This is nothing new. Jesus addressed the issue among His own followers to the extent that He taught others to not pray like the religionists of that time who thought that God would hear them because of their eloquence, or like those who prayed just to be heard by others. (Matthew 6:5-8) We still contend with the same enemies of prayer today. My prayer is that the Holy Spirit fill us, empower us, and lead us into dynamic praying!

Wanting to experience the kind of prayer that could change a city, I began early in our ministry to seek God to dramatically improve the city to which He had called us. The people of our church were only few in number, but we had great expectations. We believed that God wanted to change our city and that we could be part of that change. We spent hours in prayer and intercession over the city for some time, believing that we would reap the benefits if we did not grow weary. (Galatians 6:9) While in prayer over the city on one specific occasion, I felt impressed upon by the Lord to ask a man in the church if he would join me in prayer for the city. He agreed, and while in prayer together, we sensed the Lord directing us to drive around the city seven times. We started our prayer journey at sundown one evening, believing that we were following the leading of the Holy Spirit and that God would hear our prayers for the city. We stopped at

Chapter 3 – Prayer Dynamics

various spots along the way to pray. We stopped near the campus of a large university in the city and prayed that God would bring revival to the students of that campus and that He would break the power of drug addiction from the students ensnared with drugs. We continued into the late hours of the night until we had completed the seven rounds.

As we traveled around the city, we came to a place just inside the city limits where we felt led to stop and pray. We were on the shoulder of a major highway and had room to stand safely outside our vehicle to pray. It was a late night, and this was on one of our last trips around the city. As it turned out, we were also in front of a house where a self-proclaimed, practicing witch lived. We began to pray, not against the people in the house, but against the spirit of witchcraft working through this individual which we believed was operating contrary to the will of God in our city. We based our prayers on Scripture and asked the Lord to change the hearts of the occult practitioners or to move them out of the city. Suddenly, as we were praying, blood-curdling screams started coming from that house. As we glanced toward the house, we could see what appeared to be an entire family standing at the open screen door to the home. A female continued screaming unintelligibly. Although our hearts raced wildly, we continued to pray as she continued to scream. Finally, her screaming stopped, and we felt that we had accomplished the prayer we were sent there to pray.

A couple of days later, we drove back to the area where the professed witch lived. Upon close observation, it appeared that the house was empty. We went to a convenience store

Chapter 3 – Prayer Dynamics

across the road and inquired about the people who lived in that house. The store proprietor told us that it seemed odd to him, but that those folks had only recently moved into that house. And then he said, "I don't know what happened, but a couple of days ago, they packed their belongings and as suddenly as they had shown up, they left." He went on to say that they had stopped at his business on the way out of town and said something to the effect that they were going to California. That was two days after our prayer meeting. We were assured that our prayers had been heard and that God was using our prayers as a means of influence in our city. Keep in mind, these were not soulish prayers prayed at people, but rather prayers of appeal to the heart of God for our city.

We then made a few stops in areas of the city we knew to have spiritual strongholds. These were places where one could easily sense the powers of darkness at work. The first such stop we made was in the heart of the city. A building had been recently purchased there and opened as an XXX-rated theater. We knew in our heart that the pornography being made readily available to the youth of our community was not the plan God had for our city. We walked back and forth in front of the little theater praying that God would bring about change. We believed that the owners could have a change of heart, show clean movies, and that all those involved, both in promoting and attending these movies, would come to a real knowledge of holiness and righteousness through Jesus. Our prayers were not vindictive, mean-spirited, or directed at people. We were merely asking God to establish His will in our city. In other words, we prayed, "Your Kingdom come, your will be done." Within a short time, the theater went out of business. Another merchant moved into that building, and the atmosphere in that area of the city was noticeably changed for the better. We knew God heard our prayers and our prayers had influenced an outcome to the Glory of God.

For months after that prayer journey, visitors to the city would comment on how they felt a difference in what they sensed entering the city limits now as compared to what they had detected in past times. These people didn't know about our prayer journey, but God confirmed to us on numerous occasions that our prayers had not only been influential, but that He had moved in our city in a powerful way. These answered prayers became a testimony to God's faithfulness to influence the atmosphere of a city.

Chapter 4

Dynamic Relationships

Relationships can be incredibly complex. The effects of relationships can be either positive or negative, good or bad, meaningful or casual, but sometimes our relationships become a reflection of who we are. We all have relationships in varying degrees with others. Even casual relationships can make a lasting impact on our lives. I once had a man staying in our home who was known to have an exceptionally strong prayer life. He would be up at different times of the night and early morning praying fervently. We had heard through mutual friends of some of the dramatic results of this man's prayers. Just his very presence in our home charged the atmosphere with an expectancy of God answering prayer. Our relationship with this man was brief but the impact his relationship made on us was eternal.

The first and most significant relationship for a Christian is found in their relationship with God, His son Jesus, and the Holy Spirit. Without entering a personal relationship with Jesus, we have no promise of eternity with God. The very term, "eternal life" represents a dynamic. While true that we

Chapter 4 – Dynamic Relationships

will spend eternity somewhere, Heaven is the eternal home for believers. Salvation is not only defined by what we have been delivered from, but also clearly identifies our eternal destiny. In other words, salvation means more than just missing hell and eternal judgment. It means living in eternity in the presence of the Almighty, Creator of heaven and earth, free from all the consequences of sin, death, and judgment. Is it any wonder that Satan, our adversary, seeks to destroy our relationship with God? Lucifer (now known as Satan), sinned against God, was cast out of God's presence because of pride and rebellion and from that time until now, he has sought to bring the same consequence of the separation of man from God to all humanity. Adam and Eve sinned against God and were cast out of the Garden of Eden. While this physical separation was serious, what was even more serious was that they were now in a broken relationship with God. Sin is a separating factor between God and man. We cannot be in right relationship with Him and knowingly continue in sin. To be restored to a right relationship with God, we must follow His order. God's redemptive plan was designed to restore those who believe in an intimate, personal relationship with our Heavenly Father forever. It is because of Jesus' redemptive work of grace and provision for eternal life that our relationship with God has been restored.

Another example of a significant relationship is that of marriage. A godly marriage provides an excellent illustration of a dynamic relationship. Marriage is not only a sacred institution, but a dynamic relationship, founded in a mutual covenant before God and man. The vows made are intended to be until we are parted by death. I've heard marriage

Chapter 4 – Dynamic Relationships

partners exclaim, "We just don't seem to have the fire we used to have." Again, not addressing a physical aspect of the relationship, what does someone making that statement mean? Perhaps they mean their love for one another has grown cold. Or perhaps, there has been a mutual loss of respect. Obviously, there are many external factors such as financial crises, conflicting priorities, occupational choices, sicknesses, or a host of other outside influences which can have a detrimental impact on a marriage relationship. When the sacred vows of marriage are made, individuals agree in covenant before God and man to a mutual protection and preservation of relationship, "for better or worse, in sickness and health, for richer or poorer, until death do we part." While not everyone uses those exact words, the intent behind the vows remains the same. That means that our commitment to those vows are dynamic. Those words, when believed and enacted, provide the energy, force, and motion for a marriage until the relationship is altered by death. Even after death, the survivor may continue in the strength of the dynamics of that relationship until they, themselves, pass into eternity.

Unity in Relationships

The key to any successful relationship is unity. The Bible poses the question as to whether or not two people can walk together and not be in agreement? (Amos 3:3) Jesus, in his teachings, made a vital point, saying that if any two people can be in agreement, they can have what they ask of the Heavenly Father. (Matthew 18:19) The word "agree," by Greek definition, means to symphonize, and is the same root for the word, symphony. Jesus expressed His desire for unity

Chapter 4 – Dynamic Relationships

among God's people openly. In an amazing statement, Jesus said that the glory the Father gave to Him, He gave to His disciples that they may be one, even as He and the Father are one. (John 17:23) A very important truth that is found in those words. He has already bestowed His glory upon us that we may be one, even as He is one with the Father. The glory of the Church can be found in our walking in the glory of unity already available to us, but disunity among God's people robs God of the glory He has given the church. It's no wonder that Satan seeks to bring disharmony and strife within the ranks of the Church. There is nothing dynamic about a Church or group of people who foster strife and bring disharmony. The New Testament addresses the issues which bring disunity, such as gossip, lying, stealing, and other sinful practices, which are called works of the flesh.

Vulnerability in Relationships
Relationships require a measure of vulnerability. The greater the degree of intimacy in a relationship, the greater the vulnerability that is required. Most people don't like being vulnerable. That requires one to come out of their comfort zone. Jesus clearly exhibited the greatest vulnerability ever known when He came to earth, became a man, was tempted in all points as we are, faced rejection, and ultimately a cruel death, and identified with us in our sins. All this from one who had done no wrong and who was willing to become a servant to redeem mankind from eternal punishment and judgment. The images of Jesus dying on the cross depict one of the most intimate expressions of the Gospel. The purpose of Jesus' death was redemption. As believers, we are a redeemed people. One may ask, redeemed from what?

Chapter 4 – Dynamic Relationships

Perhaps, a better question would be "redeemed to what?" To adequately answer that, one must realize what was lost. Before we can appreciate what we have, we must have an awareness of what we lost. What was lost in the Garden of Eden when Adam and Eve fell? Many say, innocence was lost, and to a large extent that is true. However, more than innocence was lost. Intimacy was also lost. Remember, before their fall, Adam and Eve walked with God in the garden. They communed with God daily. After their fall, they were removed from the garden, and there was no further record that they enjoyed the same intimate fellowship with God. God's redemptive plan for mankind was not thwarted, however. In the New Testament, there is a reference to Jesus calling Him the "second Adam." In essence, this means that He bought back (redeemed) everything that was lost in the fall of man to restore us to fellowship with God. He not only restored our innocence through the forgiveness of sins, but He also restored intimacy and communion with the Father. We have available to us the most intimate walk with God ever afforded to mankind. Our communion has been restored. We now have boldness to enter His presence. He walks with us and dwells in us by His Holy Spirit. We are seated with Him in heavenly places. (2 Corinthians 6:16; 1 Corinthians 3:16) (Ephesians 2:6) (Matthew 28:19-20) His plan was to restore intimate fellowship to as many as can believe.

Loss of Fellowship
At one point in my life, I experienced the loss of a sense of intimacy, fellowship, and communion with the Lord and others. I know well the personal fear, pain, and anguish that

Chapter 4 – Dynamic Relationships

lingers into sleepless nights and tumultuous days of attempting to regain spiritual ground. Years ago, I went through a series of severe personal trials which consequently resulted in my leaving active ministry for a season. I had poured my life into pioneering and establishing a new church. The church grew at a modest rate and we encountered usual obstacles no more than most new churches starting without benefactors or large budgets. We went through typical growth stages spiritually, numerically, socially, and economically, but we were making good progress. It seemed that we were going to be successful and make an impact in our community for the Lord.

During the latter part of our second year in existence, problems begin to erupt with gossip and discontent among a few church members. Finally, while my wife and I were away for a speaking engagement, a wildfire of gossip had broken out in our church. It was a couple of days before we could get back home, and by the time we arrived home, irreparable damage had been done. The church was in crisis. The few disgruntled members had started a wildfire through rumors and innuendos that could not be extinguished. People left the church and finances diminished. I felt my only option was to step aside, hoping that the associate pastor could stay and possibly salvage what was left of the church. To say that this was an excruciatingly painful situation is an understatement. I battled anger, fear, and frustrations at feeling that I needed to "suffer in silence" and not to attempt to defend myself from the pulpit. I truly believed that God would vindicate me of the false allegations, even though I felt betrayed, guilty, afraid, and alone. Not knowing what to

Chapter 4 – Dynamic Relationships

do, and knowing that I was now without an income, I did the only thing I knew to do; take care of my family. I took a secular job in Houston, Texas with someone who had compassion for me. Although I now had a job and a house to live in, I was still struggling to regain my composure. I felt (although I would not admit it) that God had not "come through" for me. At the time, I didn't recognize it as a lie of the deceiver. It seemed to me that what I believed to be true from the Word of God and what I was experiencing were in total contradiction. My confusion set me up for a downward spiral. I lost my desire to pray since I was struggling to believe that God had answered my prayers and had instead allowed our ministry to fail. In my distress, I cried out to God, "Lord, I've served you with all my heart! Why would you allow this to happen to me?" Once my communion in prayer was diminished, my intimate walk with the Lord also languished. Oh, I still loved the Lord to be sure, but I no longer had the confidence that God was calling me to walk with Him in the way I had thought He had. So, I busied myself in working and providing a living.

Healing in Relationships

My wife and I had determined that even though we didn't understand all that was going on in our lives, that we must tie a knot at the end of our rope and hang on for all we were worth. For us, that meant that we had to continue to attend church. We felt that if we totally isolated ourselves from other believers, that we might never recover spiritually. The church we attended had a loving pastor who only sought to encourage me. He never really understood my problems, and being aware of the deep agony I was in, he never brought up

Chapter 4 – Dynamic Relationships

my problems. There was, however, a common ministry bond between us. One Sunday morning, I went to the altar in front of the church to pray. I was at a loss for words to even speak to the Lord, much less this caring pastor. All I could do was weep. The pastor knelt beside me at the altar, placed his hand on my shoulder, and cried with me. He never uttered a word. I don't know how long we knelt there, but after some time, we both stood up and embraced with a brotherly hug. That was it! No words were spoken, no counsel, but just a brother willing to weep with another brother. I learned at that moment, the real meaning of "weep with those who weep." (Romans 12:15) Healing of my broken spirit started through that incident, and I shall be forever grateful to a loving pastor who was humble enough to obey God.

Life was still difficult. Feeling that I had disappointed the Lord, my family, and others, and now buried under a sense of guilt and condemnation, I spiraled even further downward. My wife was earnestly seeking to encourage me, never blamed nor condemned me, but she was fighting her own battles and trying to stay encouraged herself. I knew that she was concerned about my inability to "bounce back." I felt responsible for her pain as well as my own.

Just when I thought things couldn't get any worse, my old car broke down and I had to find another way to get to work. My job supervisor felt compassionate enough to offer me a ride to and from work each day. Although a very decent human being, this man was not a believer. I found myself sharing the Lord with him during our drive time to and from work. It wasn't long, however, until he told me that our boss

Chapter 4 – Dynamic Relationships

had told him to stop giving me a ride to and from work and informed him that if he did not, he would be fired. Our boss claimed to be a Christian! How could this be? My supervisor said to me, "If this is how Christians act, I don't want to be one!" He apologized over and over to me and offered to give me a ride to within a short distance from our workplace, hoping that the boss would not see him. I didn't want him to lose his job and tried to assure him that this was not how Christians behaved. I knew that my attitude was a positive witness to him, but once again I was devastated by cruel, unjust accusations and actions.

Finally, I hit my lowest! I was walking in the heat, on the dusty shoulder of a busy highway after a long, hard day at work. Cars were swiftly passing by and were blowing dirt in my face, and I felt that I had reached my limits. I thought to myself, "I should just end it all! Life isn't worth living anymore. I've lost self-respect, my reputation has been ruined by lies and false allegations, and nobody even cares except my wife and she deserves better than this. I've disappointed the Lord, my family, myself, and there is nothing left." At that moment, on that dusty road, I had a fantastic dialogue with God. I believed in my heart that He was saying this to me; "Do you believe that like Humpty Dumpty, I can put all the pieces in your life together again?" Additionally, I sensed Him saying, "You have a choice! It is yours to make. You can continue down the path you are headed, feeling sorry for yourself, giving into despair and self-pity, or you can choose to follow my path, which will lead you out of these trials." I replied, "Lord, I don't know how you can put the pieces together again but I would like

Chapter 4 – Dynamic Relationships

that. I want to walk in your path Lord. I want to please you and walk in close fellowship with you again." The only other thing I felt I heard from the Lord that moment was, "Okay then, follow me." Tears streamed down my dirty face, but I knew that I had just had a life-changing encounter with the Lord. I now know, looking back, that at that moment, on that dusty road, God restored my intimate communion with Him.

Restoration in Relationships
Not too long after my "dusty road" experience, I received a call from a longtime friend, who through the course of our conversation invited me to minister with him. He was actively involved in ministry to young adults and wanted to know if I would be willing to help. He was also pastoring a church and offered me opportunities to minister there as well. Within a few weeks, I left Houston and joined my friend in ministry. Things were about to change. God used him to begin a process of restoration in my life and ministry. Again, he was a faithful brother who willingly obeyed the Lord by reaching out to me in a time of crisis. After less than two years of ministry there, I returned to North Texas. Somewhat later, the door was opened, through God's provision, to again pastor the Church I had founded in that area. The rest of the story is for another book, but the end of this whole incident was that God restored me to a place of more fellowship and intimate communion with Him.

Forgiveness in Relationships
It was a couple of years later that an unusual incident occurred. I had been to a men's retreat in South Texas. I left

Chapter 4 – Dynamic Relationships

the retreat early on Saturday morning because I had obligations in North Texas later that day. I drove approximately thirty-five miles from the retreat center and decided to stop at a fast-food restaurant for a quick breakfast. As I was leaving the restaurant, I heard a woman's voice call out my name. As I turned, I realized that it was a woman I had pastored at the church that was destroyed through gossip. Before I could do more than politely greet her, tears began to fill her eyes, and she said, "I need you to please forgive me. I am the one who allowed the enemy to use my tongue to destroy our church." She told me that her fellowship with the Lord had not been right since the church incident. She went on to tell me of the guilt and sleepless nights she had after she recognized that the gossip had resulted in much heartache in the destruction of the church. "I didn't know how to contact you," she said, and she said that she recently had asked the Lord to please let her see me again. "Can you please forgive me?" she begged. With tears in my own eyes, I now saw what God brought full circle, not only to restore me to a right relationship with Him, and restore my relationship with a dear sister, but also to restore a tormented sister to fellowship with Him. I expressed my forgiveness to her, prayed with her, and blessed her as we parted. I never saw her again and learned that within a couple of years from that meeting at the restaurant, that she had passed into Heaven. I marveled that God would bring us together and cross our paths at the perfect moment in time. This was clearly a providential meeting. In an amazing few moments, God had put all the pieces together again!

Chapter 4 – Dynamic Relationships

If you or someone you know ever reach the point where you feel that you are out of right fellowship with God, or you are in despair or discouraged, know this: your loving, Heavenly Father knows how and when to restore you. He will work all things for your good and will perfect those things that concern you. (Romans 8:28-29) All this to make you the person He has called you to be for His glory.

Chapter 5

Dynamic Leadership

"A leader is a person you will follow to a place you would not go by yourself." --Joel Barker

In one sense, not everybody is called to be a leader; but in another sense, we are all called to be leaders, for we are all called to let our light shine so that others may see our good works and glorify our Father in heaven. (Matthew 5:16) Someone is watching and following your life whether you are aware of it or not. As we walk with God, we are leading people to also follow and walk with Him. The Apostle Paul stated this well by exhorting others to "Be ye followers of me, even as I also am of Christ." (I Corinthians 11:1 (KJV). God has raised up effective leadership throughout history. From a Biblical perspective, there are some common threads to outstanding leadership.

Chapter 5 – Dynamic Leadership

Humility

"The quality or state of not thinking you are better than other people: the quality or state of being humble." Humility is an essential characteristic of a dynamic person. One of my favorite studies of a leader from the Bible is the study of the life and call of God on Moses. Moses attempted to talk God out of a leadership role that he felt unqualified for. Moses was noted to be an extraordinary person, who was a teachable, humble man and a righteous person. Moses, like many of us today, struggled with doubt and unbelief. He offered several excuses as to why God should not be placing him in a leadership role. His first objection to the call on his life is found in Exodus 4:1 when Moses told The Lord that the people would not believe him or listen to him. When God settled that issue, Moses brought up his second objection, saying that he was not a person of eloquent speech and that he was "slow of speech." God's call was sure, however, and Moses ultimately became the great leader God had called him to become.

The notion of a call to leadership is crucial, and attempts to lead apart from the grace and call of God either fail or tend only to highlight what man can do without God. If it can be done solely with our strength, ability, or determination, we don't need God. He doesn't want the credit for it because without Him we can do nothing, and yet, with His help, we can do anything He asks of us.

I can remember well when I knew God had called me to ministry. I was a police officer at the time and was very content with my career until God started revealing to me His

Chapter 5 – Dynamic Leadership

call on my life. After months of struggling with the call on my life, I finally bowed my heart in prayer and I reminded the Lord of the fact that I had dropped out of high school debate class because I was terrified to stand in front of twelve other students to give an extemporaneous speech. My lack of self-esteem and sense of inferiority was not humility. Humility was realizing that what I could not do, God could do with and through me. (2 Corinthians 12:9-10)

After offering all his excuses as to why he was not a capable leader, Moses consented to God's purpose in calling him to lead His people. God had not told Moses, "You Are," but rather said, "I AM" (Exodus 3:14). One of the most important steps to becoming a dynamic leader is to realize that He is the very dynamic of all that He has called you to become and do. God gives us space to either justify or condemn ourselves before Him. It seems the height of man's pride is to think that we can exalt either our "goodness" or our "badness" against God's standard of righteousness. Major W. Ian Thomas wrote, "True godliness leaves the world convinced beyond a shadow of a doubt, that the only explanation for you, is...Jesus Christ...to whose eternally and unchanging and altogether adequate 'I AM!' your heart has learned to say with unshatterable faith, 'Thou ART!'" Modern teaching has emphasized who we are in Christ, and while that is important to know, perhaps an even more significant emphasis should be on who He is in us. As with Moses, every good leader needs a burning bush experience. This event brought Moses a stark awareness to distinguish between what is common and what is holy. (Exodus 3:5) This lesson is still important for godly leaders today. Like

Chapter 5 – Dynamic Leadership

Moses, we need to come to the realization that apart from His holiness, we will not become a dynamic spiritual leader. To separate between the secular and the sacred and embrace such reflects true humility.

Conviction

Conviction can be described as a resoluteness in a strong belief one adopts and by which they remain unwavering. Convictions must not be confused with one's preferences. People's preferences can change, but a true conviction will not.

A Biblical account of a young King over Judah is given in 2 Chronicles, chapter 34. Josiah was only eight years old when he began to reign, but Scripture states that he not only did what was right in the sight of the Lord, but that even while he was young, "He began to seek after the God of David." (2 Chronicles 34:3) He followed his convictions with decisive action. Josiah had a passion for God and he initiated and enforced reforms on the people of Judah. Josiah broke down the altars of false gods, repaired the Temple of God, re-introduced the word of God as had been given to Moses, and made a covenant before the Lord to walk after the Lord with all his heart. Josiah's personal legacy, which defined him as a dynamic leader, is found in 2 Chronicles, where it is noted that he made everybody serve the Lord. He had the conviction that allowed him to lead people in a Godly way, which helped make him a dynamic leader.

Chapter 5 – Dynamic Leadership

Courage

Courage can be partially defined as a quality of mind or spirit that enables a person to face difficulty or danger with bravery and resoluteness. The Bible provides us with many examples of courageous individuals who remained steadfast and unwavering in their faith even in the face of persecution, imprisonment, and for some, loss of life. Hebrews chapter recounts the stories of some of those whom we consider to be heroes of the Faith.

After the death of Moses, Joshua was appointed to lead God's people. The first chapter in the Book of Joshua reveals specific instructions given by the Lord to Joshua. The Lord commanded Joshua to be strong and courageous, to not be terrified, and further, to not be discouraged. (v.9) This was God's charge to Joshua as he prepared to lead the people through many perils and adversities. God, in His foreknowledge, knew that the leader of His people must be one of courage. As we follow the account of Joshua and other men and women of courage in the Bible, we find that they often inspired courage in those that followed them. It takes a person of courage to encourage others. A discouraged leader cannot effectively encourage followers. While serving in the U.S. Navy, I once had the experience of going through a powerful typhoon in the Pacific. For three days, our ship was battered by both wind and massive waves. It was hardly possible to move about, and one hardly felt like eating or sleeping. As we entered that typhoon in response to a merchant ship distress signal, our Captain gave the crew notice over the public address system that we were headed into rough seas. He went on to assure us that he was confident that we would make it through this storm. There was something reassuring in his voice and demeanor. The crew picked up on his confidence. Until we were safely out of that storm, the Captain would regularly broadcast his reassurances. It was his courage that inspired us. We did come through, and many enlisted crew recognized what a courageous leader our Captain was.

Courage isn't validated until it's tested. Like schoolyard children, we sometimes espouse non-existent courage, hoping that nobody calls our bluff. Secretly, we know that we've offered an empty boast. If, perchance, someone did call our bluff, we faced the next decision, which is what has come to be termed, "fight or flight." In other words, our courage, or lack thereof, will be proven.

The young shepherd David was another who comes to mind when I think of courage. David had experienced several instances of defending his father's sheep, once from a lion and another from a bear. However, one of the courageous things for which David is probably most remembered was his encounter with the giant named Goliath. A familiar story to most, David stood in front of this giant who had intimidated the army of Israel. Armed with only a sling and some smooth stones, David challenged the one who had struck terror in the hearts of many. Most importantly, God was with David. We find encouragement for ourselves in the Scripture, which states, "...if God be for us, who can be against us?" Romans 8:31 (KJV). King David's life was a testimony to the faithfulness of God honoring a man of courage. As we face our giants, may we, like David, stand tall,

Chapter 5 – Dynamic Leadership

square-off with our enemy, knowing that God is with us, and defeat the enemy. Remember, you "… can do all things through Christ" Philippians 4:13 (KJV).

There were other great leaders who exemplified a surrendered life to the glory of God. Some of these leaders were educated, and some were not. Some were of noble birth, but not many. Some were mere children, and some were aged. Some were men, and some were women. They came from many walks of life including shepherds, fishermen, artisans, carpenters, servants, and warriors. God is still looking for those who will boldly declare, "Not my will Lord, but yours be done!" He is calling for dynamic leaders from many diverse backgrounds.

Chapter 5 – Dynamic Leadership

Chapter 6

Dynamic Faith

God will not act upon His Word on our behalf until we act upon it, for His Word does not exist for His benefit, but ours.
(Unknown)

The above statement is a thought provoking one. How do we act on God's Word? By believing it! That is faith in action. The longest chapter in the Bible extensively addresses the importance of God's Word in our lives. The chapter speaks of hiding His word in our heart, of young men taking heed to His Word, of His Word being a lamp unto our feet, and many other references to the benefits of His Word in our lives. (Psalm 119) Other passages tell us that it is impossible to please God without faith and that faith comes by hearing the Word of God (Hebrews 11:6, Romans 10:17 KJV).

The Bible contains many stories of ordinary people who became extraordinary people because of their faith. God used ordinary people to accomplish amazing things for His glory. The struggle to have faith is nothing new. The curse of sin, doubt and unbelief have plagued humankind ever since Adam and Eve were cast out of the Garden of Eden.

Chapter 6 – Dynamic Faith

The good news is that Jesus came to not only redeem us from our sin, but to restore our relationship to our heavenly Father. This entire journey is one of faith, so it is no wonder that the enemy of our soul whose stated mission is to kill, steal, and destroy, is out to rob you of your faith. We are familiar with natural laws, physical laws, and moral laws, but we sometimes overlook the fact that there are spiritual laws. Faith or trust in God and in His Word is a "spiritual law." It is that law which believes that God's Word is true and He will do what He said He would do. The Psalmist declared that heaven and earth could pass away, but not God's Word. It will remain true forever. That is foundational to a walk in faith.

For us to please God, we must have faith, and to have faith we must have the Word of God. To attempt living a dynamic faith life or life that is pleasing to God by any other standard is doomed to failure. Realizing the importance of faith, it is our responsibility to understand not only what God's Word sets forth as guiding principles in our lives, but to understand how to walk in faith according to His plan for our lives.

For the first several years of our ministry, most sermons I gave were in one way or another centered around the subject of and importance of faith. As a young pastor, I knew that we would never be successful as individuals or as a church body without faith. At the time, what became known as "faith teaching" was just beginning to be a major topic in many churches. Faith teaching spread rapidly around the world. The faith message changed forever the landscape of religion, even though there were some teachings that were

Chapter 6 – Dynamic Faith

out of balance in that message. The notion of walking in doubt, fear, and unbelief was challenged by the message of faith. This faith message made a tremendous impact on multitudes, bringing many to a new level of walking in faith and believing God in ways they had never before experienced.

As a fledgling congregation, we began to see God working in our midst in supernatural ways and with signs and wonders. It was during this time that I felt the need to get out on the street and walk in a new level of faith. I believed that if, in fact, faith was what I believed it to be, it had to work outside the four walls of the church. At least, if I was going to preach a faith message, I felt I had to be able to do so from experience. I felt I had to practice what I preached.

In the city where I pastored, there are two major universities. In my early ministry, I had a passion for reaching college students for the Lord. I spent hours just walking around the campus and talking to people, trying to get a sense of how to go forward with a campus outreach ministry. Near the campus was a café that was owned, at that time, by a man who was known as the "Campus Communist." I previously had an encounter with this man which had resulted in him becoming a Christian. Afterward, I frequented his café, and over time, we developed a strong friendship. Many days I would go to the café and pray while looking for opportunities to share the Lord with people. Often, the restaurant owner would bring people to the table where I was sitting, and often without any form of introduction, he would leave them at my table. I listened carefully for what the Lord wanted me to

Chapter 6 – Dynamic Faith

say, or what He wanted me to do. I ministered to many people in that little café, and God showed His faithfulness to others and myself many times. I began to get a reputation as "The Preacher," and it wasn't long before I had developed a ministry entirely centered around the campus.

One morning while having coffee at the café, I noticed a young man who appeared to be college age standing in the middle of a busy intersection just outside the café. He was yelling loudly enough to get the attention of anyone within a city block. The proprietor of the restaurant, realizing that something needed to be done so the young man would not be arrested for disorderly conduct, went out into the street, took him by the arm, and brought him into the café. He marched the young man to my table and said to him, "Dave, this man is a preacher. Listen to him and he will help you." With that, he turned and walked away, leaving me to talk with Dave. It took some time for me to calm him down enough so that he could speak coherently. Finally, he told me that he was very upset because he had been at a party the night before and while at the party, someone had stolen his puppy. As his story went, he had been picked up on the campus and taken to a mobile home outside the city by people he didn't know. The attraction to the party was that everybody planned to get high on drugs and alcohol. According to his account, that's exactly what they did. He had taken the puppy with him and had secured his puppy on a leash tied to a corner post of the mobile home porch. This young man was so "high" that when his new acquaintances brought him back to the campus and dropped him off in the early hours of the

Chapter 6 – Dynamic Faith

next morning, he had not noticed that they did not bring his puppy.

I asked him where the mobile home was located. He said, "Man I don't know. I'm not from here, and I have no idea where this place is. I don't know nobody, dude. All I know is they stole my dog." Well, I didn't know what to do for him, but he apparently needed the Lord. I made a few feeble attempts to witness to him, but it was falling on deaf ears. Suddenly, I opened my mouth without thinking and said to him, "Listen, I am a minister. I know a God who answers prayers, and He loves you." He responded, "If He loves me, can He help me get my puppy back?" I replied, "If we pray and God helps us find your dog, would you be willing to give your heart to Jesus?" Never would I have thought of making an offer like that. Without hesitation, he replied, "Sure dude, if God cares enough to help me find my dog, I can believe he cares 'bout me." I, now knowing that I had just put my faith on the line, said "let's pray." I prayed a simple prayer asking God to help us find his dog, and I reminded him and the Lord that this man's soul was at stake.

Dave was clueless concerning the location of the mobile home. He only knew what it looked like if he saw it, and he knew that it was somewhere in the county outside the city limits. Armed with only a sense that somehow God really cared about this young man, I continued to pray for supernatural assistance. Responding only to promptings by the Holy Spirit, I wound my way through the city and headed toward a mobile home park that I knew to be about ten miles from town. As I pulled into the large mobile home park, I

Chapter 6 – Dynamic Faith

asked him if he saw anything that looked familiar. "No," he said, "I don't recognize anything." I continued to drive through the park however, and suddenly he yelled, "There it is! That's the house." Without giving me time to stop my vehicle, he bailed out, ran up to the door, and without as much as a knock on the door, he ran inside. I had many thoughts running through my mind. I had no idea who lived there, whether they were violent, or whether this was actually the right house or not. Therefore, I did not get out of my car and kept the car engine running just in case he came running back as quickly as he had exited.

Several minutes passed, and while he was inside, I noticed a marijuana plant growing next to the porch of the mobile home. This only heightened my sense of awareness, and I was feeling a sudden urge to leave the area. While I was contemplating what to do next, my passenger came tearing out of the house with another man fast behind him.

At that point, I was thinking I really had a critical situation in the making. The owner of the mobile home suddenly came to a stop and began staring at me as though he knew me from somewhere. He said to me, "Hey man, I'm sorry! We didn't mean any harm." I wasn't sure if he had recognized me from my previous law-enforcement days or if God had just somehow made him keenly aware that he needed to pay attention to me. At any rate, I seized the moment. As I was speaking to him, I made obvious glances toward the marijuana plant. He was obviously nervous. He told us that he had returned Dave's belongings to him. And now, Dave was beginning to get the idea that something unusual was

Chapter 6 – Dynamic Faith

happening. He said, "Man, they still didn't give my dog back!" Feeling somewhat emboldened by the reaction of the man whose home was entered, I spoke with authority and asked where the dog was. He told me that the dog was not far away and that if I would come back in a couple of hours he would have it there. I said emphatically that I would be back to get the dog and that he had better not be lying to me because I would find him if he didn't keep his word. He assured me that he was telling the truth.

I took Dave back to the café and told him to stay put until I returned and I would take him to get his dog. He asked me if I really believed the man would have his dog there. By now, my faith was running high, and I said, "Yes, I think your dog will be there. Don't forget the promise you made me by giving your heart to Jesus if He found your dog." He assured me he had not forgotten that part. I left to take care of other business and as the two hours drew near, I headed back to pick Dave up at the café. We headed back to the mobile home, and as we approached it, we could see that his puppy was tied to the front porch just as it had been the night before. He gleefully jumped out of the car to get the pup. While he was retrieving the dog, I had to chuckle to myself. The mobile home appeared to be empty, and the marijuana plant was gone as well. Dave stuck his head in the door of the mobile home and exclaimed, "Wow, dude! It looks like they moved out." The happy ending was when I took him back to the café and sat in the booth with him while he loved on his puppy. By now, we had the attention of everybody in the restaurant with the amazing story of how we even found the place he had been the night before. He was telling the

Chapter 6 – Dynamic Faith

story to anybody who would listen, and he hadn't even given his heart to the Lord yet. I had the privilege of praying with Dave, who kept his promise to give his heart to Jesus. Numerous people were touched in the café that afternoon. For me, it was an affirmation of God honoring my faith to step out and believe Him for the extraordinary. Not only had a soul come to Salvation, but my faith had exploded to a new level as well.

I always had an expectancy that God was going to meet with me on the University Campus and I enjoyed spending time there. Each day was an adventure. I was aware that there was a spiritual void on the campus and set about asking God to show up there. Each day, my faith seemed to increase as God began to answer my prayers. The area of the campus where I had ministered to the young man in the café was also a haven for illegal drugs, crime, and student revelry. I knew that it would take God to change the campus environment. I prayed specifically that God would give me a key to praying a prayer of faith for the campus. The key that He gave me was on the university campus. One day, I found myself in conversation with one of the leading sellers of drug paraphernalia in the community. I had also seen him at the corner café on occasion, but had never met him. He told me that he had heard some stories about things that had happened when I prayed for some people on the campus. He obviously wasn't familiar with Scripture, and seemed awkward at asking questions. What he basically wanted to know was if God was real and did God really do the things that he had heard about. I assure him that God was real, and as matter of fact, wanted him to know the love of God.

Chapter 6 – Dynamic Faith

Though somewhat dubious, he told me that he would think about what I had said. Over the course of the next few weeks, this man would engage me in conversation as I passed his business. Finally, he told me that he wanted to know Jesus like I did and asked if I would pray for him. I had the privilege of praying with him for salvation, and shortly thereafter was able to pray with his wife as well. God had again honored my faith and the atmosphere on the Campus was changing. God still had wonderful events planned for the campus.

One Sunday morning just as I was about to preach, the drug paraphernalia seller and his wife showed up for the service. Although they had been saved, they had continued in their illicit business. The Lord touched their hearts during the service and the people of our church rejoiced to see what God was doing for people on the campus. The couple asked me if I could come by their business the next week, which I agreed to do. I dropped by their business early one morning and went inside to talk with them. The owner's wife wasn't there, but he wanted to talk. He told me how he had felt so good while at church, but when he came back to his business, he felt "down and depressed." I quickly prayed under my breath while he was assisting a "client" and asked the Lord for wisdom. When we were alone again, I asked him to follow me outside. He came out into a beautiful, sunny morning. There was fresh air, singing birds and a peaceful morning underway. I asked him to tell me what he felt at the moment. He said, "I feel light and freedom." I asked that he now follow me back into his shop, which he did. "How do you feel now?" He hesitated briefly and said, "I feel dirty and

Chapter 6 – Dynamic Faith

depressed again." I explained to him that he had just had a demonstration from God. I taught him that the Holy Spirit was not dwelling in his place of business, but that when he stepped out, he could obviously sense God's presence again. He decided to test this, so he commenced walking in and out of his business several times. He was astonished that he could tell a remarkable difference each time he experimented. I didn't want to overthrow his young faith, but told him to pray about what he had just experienced. He did just what I asked, and God sovereignly moved in his life. It wasn't long until I heard that he and his wife had been so moved by God that, much to the disdain by some of their friends, they sold their business. I never saw them again, but kept up with them indirectly for a number of years. As it turned out, he and his wife went into evangelistic ministry. The last I heard of them, he was speaking at youth crusades around the nation and many young people had come to know the Lord through his testimony and ministry. Once again, God had honored my prayer of faith.

Breaking Mediocrity

Breaking Mediocrity

Epilogue

The personal stories I've shared in this book are a remembrance to me, and my purpose in sharing is that they may be an encouragement to go forward to all who read them. To remember, serves as a catalyst or urging to go forward. The story in the Bible that illustrates this point is found in the Old Testament Book of Joshua. God had just provided a great miracle for the Israelites by bringing them across the Jordan River, which was at flood stage, with no seemingly possible way across. But God miraculously brought them across. Interestingly, Joshua commanded the people to take stones across the river with them. He went on to explain to them that the stones were to be stacked on the other side. This, he said, would serve as a memorial, or a place of remembrance. He told them that future generations would ask their fathers what these stones meant. Their answer would be that the stones were a memorial to the Lord, who, through His covenant presence with them, allowed them to cross the river by holding back the flood waters. Joshua told them this memorial would be forever.

This memorial served as a means of encouragement to future generations. Perhaps you have never thought of encouraging others from the perspective of sharing what God has done for you, but that is your story. Everybody has a story from their life that can bless and encourage others. My hope is that you are encouraged with God's faithfulness to you. Call to remembrance His blessings, favor, and miracles in your life.

Make these memories a part of your testimony. Carry your stones of remembrance with you. Build a memorial in your heart. Tell your children, friends, and acquaintances what those stones mean to you. Encourage them to build a memorial with stones from their life as well.

Those living in the past, perhaps even filled with vain regrets over their past, suffer from a loss of perspective and have lost their ability to move forward. The sort of remembrance we are talking about here serves as fuel to move forward into the future with hope, faith, and enthusiasm. The Apostle Paul declared that the one thing he was going to do was to forget the past and reach forward to lay hold of what God had in his future. (Philippians 3:13) He was stretching out to grasp what God had for him. We need a clear perspective, knowing that God, in His faithfulness to us, has not only seen us through fiery trials, but has conquered our greatest foe through His death on the cross. The cross and the empty tomb are memorials forever to the amazing grace God bestowed upon us by providing eternal life for all who believe.

Breaking Mediocrity

Breaking Mediocrity

About the Author
Gary D. Adams, D.Lit., MA, CMAS

Dr. Gary Adams is an author, a contracted public speaker for Mike Rodriguez International, LLC and a minister. He is the Vice President and Director of Education for the University of Israel Theological Seminary (UITS). He has a passion for educating and training leadership in both corporate and ministry organizations. He has specialized in teaching Bible, Emergency Management and disaster response/recovery both nationally and internationally. He began teaching emergency management from a Christian worldview while a faculty member at Ecclesia College in Springdale, Arkansas.

He has been involved for forty-eight years in active ministry, many of those years as a pastor, and in foreign and domestic missions. He has experience in the administration of faith-based agency development and effective execution of humanitarian aid programs. He has experience in disaster relief work and provision of humanitarian assistance throughout the Americas, Mexico, Europe, and Asia.

His broad background includes law enforcement and federal disaster assistance. Dr. Adams held press credentials in the 1980's and participated in radio and television talk shows on Central American affairs. He served on the Board of Governors for the American Coalition of Traditional Values (ACTV) with Dr. Tim LaHaye. He is a Senior Consultant in Emergency Management for Alpha Omega Solutions, LLC

(AOS), a security consulting company providing solutions for all aspects of global security concerns.

Dr. Adams and Ruth, his lovely wife of 53 years reside in North Central Texas. They have three grown children, fourteen grandchildren, and one great-grandchild.

Contact Gary Adams at

www.GaryAdamsInternational.com

Breaking Mediocrity

Breaking Mediocrity

Breaking Mediocrity

Disclaimer & Copyright Information

Some of the events, locales, and conversations have been recreated from memories. In order to maintain their anonymity, in some instances, the names of individuals and places have been changed. As such, some identifying characteristics and details may have changed.

Although the author and publisher have made every effort to ensure that the information in this book was correct at press time, the author and publisher do not assume and hereby disclaim any liability to any party for any loss, damage, or disruption caused by errors or omissions, whether such errors or omissions result from negligence, accident, or any other cause.

All quotes, unless otherwise noted,
are attributed to the respective Author or to the Holy Bible.

Cover illustration, book design and production
Copyright © 2017 by Tribute Publishing, LLC
www.TributePublishing.com

Scripture references are copyrighted by www.BibleGateway.com
which is operated by the Zondervan Corporation, L.L.C.

Breaking Mediocrity

Breaking Mediocrity

Breaking Mediocrity

Breaking Mediocrity

NOTES

NOTES

www.ingramcontent.com/pod-product-compliance
Lightning Source LLC
Chambersburg PA
CBHW021130300426
44113CB00006B/367